The Killdeer

And Other Stories

From the Farming Life

Even after dark, if you are quiet and attentive, you can hear a Killdeer far off. Sandbars, mud flats and grazed fields are where you find them. They are common place. So much so, that you might miss them if not for the unique sound they make as they fly overhead, or dart back and forth on the ground, as if they are wondering which way to go next. So it is with Michael Cotter's stories. They are like a comfortable pair of slippers. Not flashy at all, but each time you put them on and walk in them, you are so glad you did. They are so ordinary, but the way they wrap around your soul surprises you. And like slippers you thought you'd never buy, Michael's stories surprise you. Even though they are not flashy, energetic or dramatic in ways we have come to expect in this digital age, they are grounded in universal truths, with characters that are timeless. They provide us with a sense of memory, wisdom and peace that celebrates the human spirit, and revels in the common man, woman, boy and girl that is in us all. When Michael tells his stories, it's as if time stands still. We are reminded of who we really are … down deep … after the television is turned off, the radio is silenced, and we have put our egos on the shelf to rest a spell.

—**Rex Ellis**, Director of Museum Programs, Smithsonian Institution, a Circle of Excellence storyteller of the National Storytelling Network and Author

"When Michael Cotter shares a tale, you can see the sun rising over fields. You can hear the cattle chorus and feel the cool mud of the barnyard beneath your feet. Michael Cotter brings spirituality to observations of daily life." —**Judith Black**, Circle of Excellence Storyteller and Recording Artist, Boston, MA area

In 1984 Michael posed for his first professional storytelling picture. It was under this windmill in the 1930s that the hoboes shared their stories.

The Killdeer

And Other Stories
From the Farming Life

Michael Cotter

Honored by his peers as a Circle of Excellence Storyteller
of the National Storytelling Network

Parkhurst Brothers Publishers
MARION, MICHIGAN

www.parkhurstbrothers.com

Parkhurst Brothers books are distributed to the trade through the Chicago Distribution Center, and may be ordered through Ingram Book Company, Baker & Taylor, Follett Library Resources and other book industry wholesalers. To order from Chicago Distribution Center, phone 1-800-621-2736 or send a fax to 800-621-8476. Copies of this and other Parkhurst Brothers Inc., Publishers titles are available to organizations and corporations for purchase in quantity by contacting Special Sales Department at our home office location, listed on our web site. Manuscript submission guidelines for this publishing company are available at our web site.

Printed in the United States of America
First Edition, 2014
2014 2015 2016 2017 2018   10 9 8 7 6 5 4 3 2 1

Library of Congress Cataloging in Publication Data:

Library of Congress Cataloging-in-Publication Data

Cotter, Michael, 1931-
   The killdeer and other stories from the farming life / Michael Cotter. – First edition.
      pages cm
   ISBN 978-1-62491-042-5 (alk. paper) – ISBN 978-1-62491-043-2
   1. Farm life–United States–Anecdotes. I. Title.
   S521.5.A2C67 2014
   630–dc23
                              2014016166

ISBN: Trade Paperback   978163491-042-5
ISBN: e-book   978162491-043-2

Parkhurst Brothers Publishers supports the First Amendment of the United States Constitution and believes that access to books and ideas are necessary for a people to remain free.

This book is printed on archival-quality paper that meets requirements of the American National Standard for Information Sciences, Permanence of Paper, Printed Library Materials, ANSI Z39.48-1984.

Cover photo by   Paulette Mertes
Cover and text book design: Linda Parkhurst, Ph.D.
Transcribed and edited by: Beverly Cotter
Acquired for Parkhurst Brothers by: Ted Parkhurst
Proofread by: Ben Rosenfield, Ph.D.

102014

Dedicated

to my older brother Dick

who challenged me to be more brave

than I wanted, and to dream. I didn't have a chance to tell him

that he was my hero.

Acknowledgements

Hillary Clinton once said, "It takes a village to raise a child." The same is true about a book of personal stories that come from my community. The first of those who helped me on my journey include my family: Dad who found humor in unusual places, and my sons, Marty and Tom, who took responsibility for the farm when I travelled to tell stories. Storytelling festival supporters like Mike Bednar, Joe and Martha Ott and Betty Benner, somehow believed I could be an artistic director .

Good media people at KSMQ, KAUS, and WHO—as well as regional newspapers—connected me with a wider audience. Most of all, I salute and thank the community of neighbors in and around Austin, Minnesota, who supported me and let me tell their stories nationwide.

Contents

Michael and Bev Cotter

I thought that my stories could never be written in my voice. Then I met Beverly. Her German logic, my Irish way, and our mutual love of words blended. With that understanding and trust came a dream. She questioned, "Why can't these stories be written?" Then, she picked up her pencil and asked, "Michael, will you tell me a story?" Thanks to her determination and talent, my stories will live on in the written word.

—Michael Cotter

A Farmer and a Storyteller

"Cut out those damn stories and get some work done around here!" That was my most dreaded message from my dad. Our farm was a livestock farm and it was pretty labor intensive in the early years. There were two or three hired men around all of the time. Some were hoboes who drifted in looking for food and work and shelter, and others were young people coming from farms where they needed to get out and earn their own living. They lived in a bunkhouse between the house and the barn, and they ate their meals in the house with the family. Mealtime was a time of relaxation and that was when the more humorous side of my dad's personality would come through. He could be quite entertaining.

Our farm was a mile in every direction from any other farm, so there were not any neighbor kids to play with. My brother was older, a hard worker and very quiet, but we were still good friends. I really liked animals. Even though they were going to market eventually, they were my pets. Except for the school year, that was the extent of my companions.

My dad was fifty-five years older than myself, and very much the manager of that farm. He believed that everyone should be doing work that matched his size and age. I was always interested in people and wanted to get to know them, and I guess I liked to talk. Dad would often interrupt me with that, "Cut out those stories…," statement, and it always made me feel a little put down and embarrassed.

If I would complain to him or be offended, his way of handling it would be to say, "Mike, you're a nice young fella, but you are such a damn old hen of a man." He meant I should not take insults or put-downs personally, I should just be able to let them roll off my back.

His announcement reminded me of my place: that I had a responsibility for the well-being of the farm: that I was not like those other men; that my dad was not a young man, and it was up to me to assume some of the responsibility. My job was not to interfere with their work, but to use my energy to sort of manage and help us be more efficient.

We traveled very little when I was young, and I loved hearing the stories of these people whose lives were so very different from mine, and the routes they had traveled before we met. Some were war veterans—and they were often alcoholics. I had to learn to not be afraid, but to stay away from them when they were angry. Yet, they wanted to share their stories. Some were just a few years older than me, on their own for the first time in their life, trying to find their way in this big world.

The alcoholics at the end of a drunk were quite pitiful

before they could get their façade, their shield, back up. I sympathized with their pain because it seemed they really had no future. I thought my dad just didn't seem to notice the hurt feelings, or the disappointments, or the failures.

An example of that was a situation involving a man named Hank. We were putting up hay on a Saturday and it was getting close to evening. Hank wanted to get up town. We knew if he did, he would be gone for two or three days. A rain was coming and the hay needed to be put up in the barn to be protected. One more load had to be brought in from the field, but Hank was headed for the bunkhouse to get ready to go to town. Dad grabbed him and told him to get back out in the field.

I was maybe eight or nine years old at that time. It was my job to drive the horses and pull the hay loader, and Hank was to load the hay. Both of us knew how to work well together.

When we went back to work, Hank was so angry that he threw the hay right on top of me as I was trying to drive the horses. I was afraid he would push me off the wagon. Later, we had to stop and rest a while and put down the sling rope. Hank's anger was so great that all of a sudden he looked at me, furiously, and said, "I am better than this! I am better than this!"

Then, without any warning, he started talking about fighting in France and sleeping among those dead bodies; and getting up in the morning, picking up his gun and going back into battle.

I started seeing that Hank had known a life that I had

never dreamed of, and understanding, maybe a little better, why he needed to get away from life for just a little while. As time went on he started telling me more about his life. I think I knew these men in a way that my dad did not. More likely, Dad felt that his position required him to keep some distance between himself and hired hands.

I have fond memories of summer evenings, when the milking had been finished and darkness was settling. The men would be sitting under the windmill that was pumping cold water across the milk cans to cool them. Maybe there was a little fire started to keep the mosquitoes away. These men, with all their different backgrounds and life experiences, would gather and start sharing their stories. I was just fascinated with the world that they knew that I did not.

These stories were all inside of me. When I was introduced to the storytelling world, I knew I had to be a part of it. Yet, I never believed that my stories would ever be done on stage. When I started meeting with storytellers, I would tell about something that happened on the farm and someone would say, "That would make a good story." I was shocked because it was just a little incident.

When we would meet for a weekend of storytelling there was so much affirmation. I would drive home with all of these things rolling through my head and my mind would be whipping. One time, I planted corn most of the night, got up the next morning after very little sleep and headed to a storytelling weekend. I wasn't a bit tired and I knew something crazy was happening.

I began to realize that all my encounters, whether with people, animals, or machines, were potential stories. I began to see stories everywhere. The first story I told was about a little bird trying to protect her nest. I was amazed at how people listened and then shared their stories with me. Then I remembered my dad in his old age, and the old dog that was a good friend, but didn't understand Dad's sense of humor. Dad would sit on his tail, pretending it was an accident. Toby would get furious! Then, a few moments later, they would be making up and Toby would be licking his face. It was this same sense of humor that was so very helpful as we worked together when I was taking over the farm. Dad had the ability to turn a heated situation into one of laughter. It helped to ease our generational conflict.

My stories of family and farm have taken me to places I never dreamed possible. I was so surprised the day my hired man came running out of the shop, hollering, "The Smithsonian's on the phone!"

Now I have the chance to relate those stories as I remember them, and they call me a "storyteller."

The Killdeer

My name is Michael Cotter. I am a third generation farmer from Austin, Minnesota, where the land is flat and the soil is black. Many of those farms have been in the same families for a hundred years, and ours is one of those farms.

This started changing rapidly in the 1960s, and I think it was because of the introduction of the one hundred horsepower tractor. Prior to this time, the tractors ranged from twenty to sixty "horse." The biggest tractor on our farm was a fifty five horsepower machine. Then they came out with the one hundred horse, and where this doesn't sound like a big change, those wheels had to be doubled to utilize the power.

Very shortly, we were introduced to the two hundred horse, and then the three hundred horse, and even the four hundred. There didn't seem to be any limit to the power, because these were the four-wheel drives. Each tractor had eight large tires standing as tall as a man.

These large machines needed large fields, and so

drainage ditches were dug in that flat, black land. A drainage ditch is a canal ten to fourteen feet deep, where the water runs only in the bottom two or three feet in the dry season. Three feet below the ditch bank, tile lines were laid like spider webs that fanned out into the low swamp area, and the fields became larger; but many others disappeared. Other changes happened at this time. As those fields grew in size, whole farms disappeared.

If you were to drive west of Austin on Interstate 90 and look to the south, you'd see a hundred acres of very flat land. That's part of our farm. When I was a little boy, my brother and I would trap muskrats in the winter for spending money. One day I stood on what is now that field, trying to count the muskrat houses. There were so many I could not count them all.

The story I want to tell you is about one spring day, while operating a four-wheel drive tractor, I was pulling a thirty-five foot wide disc along the edge of this ditch bank, where many little stones had been brought up from deep in that earth.

Ahead of my tractor, was a bird called a killdeer. These are little land birds with small bodies sitting on top of quite long legs, and when they run they almost look like they are floating over the land.

Killdeer have a couple of special characteristics. First, their cry sounds a lot like their name. But the most noticeable trait is the way they defend their nest, which is just eggs placed among those little rocks, eggs that match the stones perfectly.

The killdeer protects her nest with drama. She acts crippled, and with a wing dragging and looking very helpless, she tries to lead the enemy away from her nest.

This spring morning, the bird in front of that big tractor began her familiar drama. First she dragged one wing, fluttering just in front of the eight big, rolling tires, trying to lead the tractor and big disc off to the side and away from her nest. Of course, with these big machines, there is nothing to do but keep going, even knowing that the nest must be near. Soon she's back again, more crippled than before. Both wings are dragging now, almost tumbling along the ground, barely staying clear of the eight big tires that are steadily rolling. Again, I have no choice but to keep going.

The bird comes a third time. This time it's different. Like life itself, the pretending is now over. She's going to take her stand. With a piercing screech I hear above the sound of the engine, she stands her ground in front of that big rig.

I slammed in the clutch and pulled the kill switch. When that big diesel engine stopped its roar, I was shocked at the silence. It became so still. I was able to hear the water running in the drainage ditch. I was even aware of the birds singing along the ditch bank. I looked down on that killdeer standing so tiny in front of the tractor. She was just looking at me and she, too, had become silent. She wasn't even as tall as the rubber lugs on those eight, big tires.

Because there was no one to make fun of me, or to question why, I said to that bird, "You have got to show me where it is." That's when the magic happened. It was like she understood. There was just a moment's hesitation, and she moved off of the corner of my tractor, spread her wings, and sat down. Defying her instincts, she showed me her nest. I restarted that diesel engine, and with the hydraulic lever brought that disc up on its transport wheels. With almost a foot of clearance, that machine rolled over the top of the bird.

Then, returning those sharp disc blades to the earth by means of the hydraulic, I opened the throttle and that black, diesel smoke rolled. Soon those wheels were moving at six miles an hour again.

I turned and looked back through the dust. I could see that square piece of untilled soil and barely spot the lone bird sitting there. I knew then that our time together was over.

Horse Trading

Dad was born in 1876. It was a pioneer time, when people made do with what they had, and it was a time of being dependent mostly upon just yourself. There were very few doctors, and even fewer lawyers, in the communities. People had home-cures and settled their own disputes.

Good horses were one of the farmer's most important possessions. He took great pride in being able to trade horses and get a better one than he traded. Consequently, there were professional horse traders, but of course the farmer wanted to be just as skilled in trading. One of the ways you proved that was to trade horses with the Gypsies. The Gypsies traveled in bands at that time, moving through the countryside, where they were feared because they stole things, and they were respected because they understood horses so well and were great traders.

Early in the 1900s my father was a young man working on our farm, and one evening he saw a band of Gypsies camping in the woods about a mile away. He knew that they always had horses with 'em and would be eager to trade.

He had a horse he wanted to trade, and he planned to do so when they traveled by in the morning. The horse he had was a nice looking grey mare, young and strong and gentle, but it had a lung problem. This occurred when horses ate moldy hay and it gave them an asthmatic condition. I don't know what the medical term is, but I heard them say, "The horse has the heaves." The symptoms would not be noticeable until the horse was pulling a load, and as it started to breathe fast or hard, there would come that whistling sound of breathing that was restricted. A horse with this condition was really almost worthless because it would have to be rested often, and it was an awful thing to hear the horse coming with that whistling sound. My dad wanted to get rid of that horse.

He made his plans very carefully. Early in the morning he had that horse hitched with another one on a cultivator. He purposely hitched it with another horse that didn't match it at all in size or build. That way he could find one that the Gypsies would have, that would match his much better.

He watched for when the Gypsy band started down the road, and had his team of horses resting at the end of the corn row that he had just cultivated. Every good farmer rested his horses. That was the thing to do. His timing was just right, because his grey horse was breathing normally and it looked like an ordinary good horse.

He and the Gypsy leader exchanged greetings when they came along, and they stopped to see if they could do some business. My Dad, of course, wanted to be pretty shrewd, and said the thought "just occurred to him at that moment" that maybe he could get a horse that matched his big horse better than the grey one did.

The Gypsies had several horses tied behind their wagon and they motioned for him to look at them, but my Dad was watching the one they were driving. He was a fine looking horse, young and strong in stature. He looked healthy, and Dad noticed that while they were talking the horse was eating the grass along the road, so he was a very gentle horse. He was just a single horse pulling the wagon, but he just seemed to be perfect in every way.

When Dad said that he would like to have the horse that they were driving, the Gypsy man said, "Oh, that would be more money." So they haggled back and forth on the price, and eventually my Dad traded the grey horse for that fine big horse. Dad's horse had to be unharnessed and the Gypsies tied it behind their wagon with the others. Then they brought up another horse from the back to hitch on to their wagon, and Dad's new horse was put in the harness beside his remaining horse on the cultivator. When they were placed together, my Dad saw they looked perfect. He had made a good deal.

Dad watched the Gypsies drive on down the road, just so pleased with himself. He had beaten the Gypsies in a trade.

He started down the row of corn with his now perfect team, but as soon as that new horse started to pull beside the other one he moved in a dog-fashioned way, walking at an angle. He could not walk straight down the row. With his front feet he was trampling one row of corn, and with his back feet he was trampling another one. Apparently, the only way that horse could pull was as a single horse. He could not work in a team. Also, because he pulled sideways, the harness didn't fit right, and it made sores along one side of his body.

The strength that he had wasn't used right, and he was no help at all, confusing the other horse. So Dad really couldn't use him.

My Dad had not had him an hour before he realized that he had gotten a much worse horse than the one he'd gotten rid of. A young man who fancied himself a good horse trader, he knew he had failed badly.

A few days later, he was driving a team of horses down the road past the Guy Farm. The Guys were neighbors with a large farm and quite a few horses. There was a certain amount of competition between our two families that I never really understood, because we were always very polite to each other and worked together occasionally. But the Guy family was from North Ireland and my Dad's family was from South Ireland.

As my dad was driving by, Mr. Guy was out cultivating corn. Even in the distance, Dad could hear the horse he had traded, with the loud whistle, that poor animal that couldn't breathe. He saw that Mr. Guy had bought the grey horse that Dad had traded to the Gypsies. He said to him, "Art, what are you doing with my horse?" Mr. Guy was a man who never swore. He was very proper. But his face was red with anger and he swore at those Gypsies, and then he and my Dad had a good laugh together. They had both sought to out-trade the Gypsies, and they had both been taken.

The Gypsies had beaten two prominent farmers, and hadn't traveled three miles to do it. They must have felt that they had a pretty good day.

My Dad always told that story on himself, and he always said it was a good thing when he and his neighbor, Art Guy, could laugh at themselves. I think they both had great respect for the abilities of the Gypsies.

Me and Dad

My Dad died in January of 1967. He was 91 years old.

We were in a new church at that time called St. Edwards. In the Catholic Church, John XXIII was the Pope. He was quite an elderly man and had very liberal ideas. In one of his first speeches he said, "We must open the windows and let fresh air blow in." It led to many changes in the church. Our new Pastor, Father Corcoran, was in favor of this more liberal atmosphere. The people in Austin who didn't want change went back to the former church, St. Augustine's, but many young couples with children joined St. Edward's. It was a wonderful time and we became a close community, almost like a family.

My Dad was the oldest member of the church and one of the few older people who seemed to like the changes, the new modern way. His death was the first one at St. Edward's and it was decided that everything would happen in the church, both the wake service and the funeral. It was a very powerful experience, because everyone was there for everything.

My Dad's casket was up in front of the altar at the wake service, and my family was all there from distant places. I had six older sisters, three of whom were nuns. The eldest, Mary Catherine, was in charge of the whole funeral, the arrangements and everything.

It seems as though that was her mission. I was amazed at the way she took charge, not knowing that in a few years she herself would die. She would be the next death. I was the youngest in the family and one of two boys. I was the one who stayed on the farm and worked with Dad, and eventually took it over. Because he was born in 1876, it had been quite a struggle to modernize the farm, although he was anxious to help and in good health with a lot of good experience to offer.

Somehow it was decided that I would speak at his wake service and funeral. He and I had shared so much joy and anger and frustration with each other. And yet, we had a great deal of respect for each other. I always enjoyed his sense of humor. It was hard to be angry with him when he said some funny things that would make me laugh.

My young family was there in church with me. We had three children at that time. As I stood up beside his casket to welcome the people, I was so filled with emotion looking down at him.

My speech went something like this: "My Dad has lived a full life. He was born and died on the farm that he loved, and he always was a voice of authority. But when he went out for an evening, he thought it should be sociable with a good lunch.

"We thank you all for coming here tonight, paying tribute to my Dad and sharing in his memory, and we invite you all to come down to the coffee room to visit and have a good lunch."

As the people filed by the casket on the way to the downstairs family room, they'd take my hand, and some, with tears in their eyes, thanked me for what I had said. Somehow all that feeling brought so many memories back. Then it was just me and Dad.

It was such a powerful experience, leaning on that casket and seeing him there so frail. I had always thought of him as strong and the voice of authority. I was really affected by the outpouring of emotion from the people in the church.

I went back to one night when the cattle got out and into the cornfield. The corn was really tall and it was dark, and Dad, my older brother and I, we were probably seven and ten years old, were in the cornfield trying to chase the cattle out of there in the dark. I was really scared. My Dad said, "Hell, spread out now so we can cover the whole field." My brother had to be the furthest away from my Dad, who kept saying, "Spread out. Don't bunch up." We were going along, and all of a sudden a cow came crashing through the corn stalks right in front of me. I moved over closer and closer to Dad until l could hear him walking and breathing, and then I felt safe. Me and Dad.

I remember the time that the storm hit our farm, and the wind shook the house. Mother was praying and making us frantic, and my Dad and older sister were trying to hold the door shut against the wind. After the wind calmed, Dad went out with the lantern to see if any buildings had blown down. It was still storming and I was scared until I heard him come back into the house. Then I felt safe again. Me and Dad.

Dad would never take any lip from any one on that farm. When I was about nineteen years old and starting to take charge of the farm, Dad was in his mid-70s. I had a forty year old man with quite a temper working for me. Just when we were so busy in the spring getting the crop in, the man insulted my dad. Dad told him he was not working there any longer, and that he should leave. I was so angry when I realized Dad had fired the man I needed, that I came in and confronted him.

We were standing in the barn and I shouted at him, "How could you do that when you know we need him so badly right now?" His response was, "No one speaks to me that way." I said, "If you weren't so old, I'd knock you flat," and I brought my hands up. I will never forget what happened. The gleam came into his blue eyes, and that half smile on his face that I had seen so often when he confronted someone. He brought his big hands up and said, "If you think you are man enough, don't let my age stop you." And then, as a final insult, he said, "Remember, better men than you have tried." I noticed how big his hands were. I had a flash of wisdom at that moment, and I got to thinking, "Who would you brag to if you did knock your seventy-five year old Dad down?" and, worse yet, "What if I lost?" I walked away. He always acted like it was no more important than if a bird had flown over. He never mentioned it again. It was just one of those things in life. Me and Dad.

I could hear the conversation in the church family room

as people visited and laughed and celebrated his life. There we were together, just the two of us again. And I said, "How am I going to get along without you? We have been together for so long. You were always out there if things didn't work right. You were my buffer in life."

I could hear my little children coming up the steps.

"I have to go now. It's been nice being here together."

Just me and Dad.

Family Values

It was during the Second World War, and I was twelve years old. There were certain values on our farm that probably wouldn't resonate in today's world. Everyone was expected to help, and no one expected to be paid for helping. There was always plenty of work to do, and because I was the younger of two boys, and as our father was older, it was assumed that one of us would be running the farm some day. We were given money only for things that our parents thought were necessary.

So, for spending money, my brother and I started trapping. A lot of the low areas on our farm had muskrat houses. We would set traps in these houses, and because muskrat pelts were worth three to four dollars apiece, it was a wonderful source of money. It involved checking the traps each day, plus taking care of our chores.

Mink pelts were worth much more than muskrats, but mink were very hard to catch. Also, a mink would chew its paw off and escape if it was in the trap very long. One day, in one of the traps, I had the excitement of finding a mink. He just about had his foot gnawed off when I came upon him. I hit him over the head with a stick several times before he died. It was hard for me to do. When I got back to the house I was very excited and asked my Dad what I should do. He suggested I take the mink to school, and during the noon hour go down to the two Jewish scrap and hide buyers to see what they would give me for it. I was in sixth grade and kind of shy.

When I took my mink down to a place called Dubinski's, I saw Mr. Dubinski, who most people called Charlie, sitting up on the top of a smelly pile of hides, skinning a muskrat. I later on learned he was a millionaire, but that day he was sitting up there with a hot plate making soup with potatoes and carrots and other vegetables. As I talked to him, he reached over with his skinning knife and stirred the vegetables, which was a shock to me.

Now, my father had told me to check with both of these businessmen, but not to sell the mink. When I asked Mr. Dubinski what my mink was worth, he looked at it carefully and said, "I'll give you three dollars and fifty cents for it," and I said, "No." When he asked me what I wanted, I made the mistake of telling him that my Dad told me not to sell it. Then he yelled at me, "Get out of here, you no good kid, and quit wasting my time." This really shook me up, but I was taught to follow orders and I went to the next place, even though I didn't want to.

There I met a younger man named Mr. Usem. He said he would give me seven dollars and fifty cents, and then he acted like I would probably sell it. Then, being kind of scared, I said that my dad told me not to sell it. He also yelled at me, but not quite as bad, and told me not to come in if I couldn't do business with him.

I went back to school pretty shaken, and I brought the mink back home. A day or so later, my father went in with the mink and talked to both of the dealers. He sold the mink for thirty-two dollars, which was very much of a shock to me.

Many years later, I was telling a retired businessman about it and I said, "I think my Dad was kinda rough on me to send me into that deal." He laughed and said, "You still remember it, don't you?"

And I said, "Just like it was yesterday."

Dad and the Spring Chicken

I graduated from high school in 1949 and started working full time with my dad. He was seventy-three, in good health, and with a strong will.

This was shortly after the Second World War ended. In 1949, to get machinery, you put your name on a waiting list, and allowed months as industry was changing over from wartime to peacetime production. Prior to that, you'd sign up on a waiting list, but never get the machine.

The farms had all been held in a state of "no progress" during, and after, the war years. There was quite a struggle going on between my Dad and myself. I wanted to modernize and get some labor-saving equipment, and he sort of had his old age planned. It would be the way it always had been, though he would not have as much work to do. He would just help. He did allow *some* change in the crop and field equipment. We could become a *little* modern there.

But in the winter, when all of the cattle and calves came

into our big barn, he wanted that scene to remain just the same as it had always been. Even though there were no more milking cows and we were raising beef cattle, the animals still stood in stanchions with all of those cows having to be fed and bedded individually.

The upper part of that barn held many, many tons of loose hay that had to all be handled by fork and carried to the different animals. On the northeast corner of that barn stood a big silo. It was in the shade of the barn, so the sun never hit it. The silage froze along the edge from December 'til April, which meant that you had to climb up, chop and pick the frozen silage from the walls, then throw it down and carry it to the cattle in a basket. One of the first pieces of labor-saving equipment I brought to that farm was the "bushel-and-a-half-basket", a switch from the bushel.

We could not move snow with anything but a shovel, because the old tractors were not of any use in the winter. So we also had to keep a team of horses in the barn to pull the wagons or the bobsled through the snow. This all made the winters long and dreary for me, with endless chores seven days a week.

One of the ways my Dad liked his retirement, was for me to get out to the barn early in the morning and start feeding those cattle. Later, about six-thirty a.m., he would come out and help. Mainly he would visit with the animals and see that they were all fine, do what little work he wanted to do, and then we both would go to the house and have a good breakfast.

After breakfast we would return to the barn, where I would spend the full day getting the silage out of the silo and getting the loose hay out of the haymow in preparation for the next day's feeding, and then doing the cleaning of the bedding for the cattle. This was an ideal situation for him, but not necessarily for me.

This particular year a chicken, born totally out of season, found her way to the warm barn. She was a beautiful little hen, almost grown, jet black with white flecks on the ends of the feathers. If there was ever a beauty contest for hens, she would have been in it.

Because she was the only chicken in a barn full of cattle, she had to stake out her territory. At first, she was in terror as baby calves ran after her up and down the alleys, and cows would bunt at her with their heads. Soon she learned how to get along, flying in the faces of those baby calves, which were then terrified of her and ran in the other direction; and she'd peck at the noses of the cows if they would bother her. It wasn't long at all 'til she just fit right in with the group, and she became very much a character.

I started noticing that my dad always whistled as he was coming toward the barn. He had a wonderful clear whistle trained from many hours of working alone in the fields.

We would hear that clear whistle coming, and then the creaking of the frosty hinges as that door opened on the horse barn to the west. The horse barn was always colder with only one team of horses standing in it, and in the darkness Dad would always speak to them as he came through. Then the whistle would carry on into the main area of the barn where the cattle were standing. Soon, I noticed that this little hen would run toward the door when she heard the whistle, and my dad always greeted her in a loud voice. He would ask her how she was and if she'd had a good night's rest. Sometimes he would even bend down to pet her, but she would sort of dance away from the petting. She didn't think that was appropriate in their relationship.

Then the two of them would go down the alleys together, greeting all the cattle and seeing that they were being well fed. That little hen would look up at him, and sometimes he would ask her kinda personal questions, like he was wondering if she'd ever thought about laying an egg. Mostly, they just walked around together, for they were good friends.

One day this little hen was just not herself. At first, he thought she was just out of sorts. Then he realized that she was getting ready to lay her first egg. He went over to a manger where the calves were eating hay. This was before we started baling hay so it was piled high in loose, fluffy mounds. In that soft hay, my dad made a deep, dark hole because he knew that laying that first egg is a big job. That little hen was standing right beside him, kinda puzzled at what he was doing. Then, without any warning, he scooped her up and put her into that dark hole he'd made in the hay.

She popped right back out of that nest. She was indignant. She thought he had stretched the bounds of their relationship. She was just ready to fly back out of that manger, when it occurred to her that it was just the spot that she was looking for. She got back into that nest. He had been right all along, and she settled down to begin the job of laying that first egg.

He would check on her from time to time, and pretty soon she was standing up on the railing, cackling and celebrating that egg. He came over to congratulate her, and she cackled happily. He laughed and they had a little celebration right there together.

Later on he took that little egg to the house where he told my mother the story of that special little hen, and she fixed that egg for his lunch.

Morning after morning, the situation was the same. The little hen would be there to greet him at the door, they would visit with everyone and do whatever work they needed to do, and later in the morning she would let him know that it was time to lay her egg.

Then he would fix a nest for her. By now, she would just hop right up in there without any hesitation. Before long she would be up on the edge of the manger, cackling, announcing a new egg, and accepting his congratulations. Before long that egg would go off to the house for my Dad's lunch.

One time, while she was trying to lay her egg, the calves were eating that hay and tossing it around with their heads. She couldn't lay her egg in that situation, so she hopped out of the nest and went right past me. She found Dad somewhere in the barn and let him know her need. Soon he was coming back with his long strides, with that little hen running beside him like a tattletale. He chased the calves away and made her a new nest. She hopped up into it, and pretty soon was announcing a new egg.

My life has changed after all these years. That little hen and my Dad are long gone. I now call myself a storyteller, and at times I tell my stories in retirement homes. I oftentimes see old men, about the age of my Dad when he was enjoying retirement by spending his days in the barn. They sit before me in clean clothes, and all their bodily needs are taken care of. But when I see their eyes, the life seems to be gone from them.

I long for them to have a big barn filled with animals that they love and a little hen waiting at the door to greet them. And, maybe later on in the morning, that little hen would jump up in the nest that they had made and lay a new fresh egg for their lunch.

South St. Paul Stockyards

I remember one really hectic night on the farm in 1935. I was a young boy about six or seven years old. It was snowing and miserable. Some cattle had come into Austin on the train and had been unloaded into pens at the railroad station. They had to be brought out to the farm. This involved hiring men with trucks that would hold six or seven head, getting the cattle loaded, and bringing them to the farm. We did not have electricity at that time, and the only areas cleared of snow were the paths we had shoveled between buildings. With lanterns and poor visibility, blowing snow, and trucks getting stuck in snowdrifts, the cattle were finally unloaded into the barn. They were thin and sick. I remember all the chaos.

My Dad had gone to St. Paul and ordered a railcar load of thirty cattle, to be purchased by a commission buyer at the St. Paul Stockyards. This was done over a period of a week and then they were shipped down to Austin by train. I had a feeling that this was something that very few farmers would do, that this was a giant undertaking.

The St. Paul Stockyards extended over a mile along the railroad. On one end were Swift, Armour, Cudahy, and some smaller packing plants, together employing thousands and thousands of people in the slaughter of animals. They processed hogs, cattle and sheep. All of these animals were bought and sold through the yards.

At that time, the livestock came into South St. Paul by train and truck. They were put in pens and sold by commission firms to the packing companies, or to dealers who had little groups of pens, who would then sell back out to the farmers who were in need of livestock.

The commission companies would represent the seller, who might be from a distant place, so he would get a fair price for his livestock.

On the other end of the South St. Paul Stockyards were the dealers who bought cattle that were not yet ready for slaughter. They also had orders for farmers who wanted to grow these cattle bigger and sell them back for slaughter. The dealers were more independent. They generally tended to be either Irish or Jewish, and I saw them as the forerunners of used car dealers, with that kind of a reputation. One could also hire the commission companies to send a professional buyer to the dealers, and purchase what you wanted at a fair price. Then you would pay a commission for that service. Hundreds of people were employed by the stockyards in these various jobs, and there were hundreds of pens holding the cattle of various owners.

When I was about 16 and my brother Dick was home

from college for the summer, he, my Dad and I went up to the stockyards where Dad bought a few cattle. Dad was about 70, and his time of dealing on our farm was nearing its end. He was wanting to slow down. In this huge stockyard, as we were walking through the alleys, the professional dealers with cowboy hats and dark glasses would try to help him decide what cattle he wanted to buy. In an arena like that, it was a "buyer beware" situation, and my Dad was an old hand at dealing. The middle-aged people selling cattle started playing to the fact that he was an older man with his two young sons. We visited several pens and looked at many cattle and talked to several salesmen. Looking back, it was as if they all seemed to know what the others were doing, as if they had a network between them. I remember them calling my Dad, "Dad," because he was there with his sons. I found myself being embarrassed at times, as my Dad couldn't seem to get a grasp of what was going on. He would like a few cattle from one pen and a few from another pen. It was a hot day and these people were shifting them around, trying to get the cattle he wanted. As they got the bunch together that he wanted, he would change his mind because the price was too high. So there was a lot of irritation and impatience, and, of course, swearing—that always went with it. But the embarrassment to me was that my Dad never seemed to understand exactly what was going on.

He would be dealing on one bunch and then turn around and be dealing on another, and the buyers were getting kind of angry. And finally, one guy just had to leave and my Dad made him an offer. He was very impatient. He wouldn't take Dad's offer because it was too cheap, and even though he was not a short man, my Dad said, "I'll tell you what, Shorty. You throw up a coin. If it comes down heads, I get them at my price. If it comes down tails, it will be the lowest price you offered." You could see the salesman was at his wit's end. He was angry and frustrated, and wanted to sell those cattle and get out of there. My Dad always was lucky with a coin toss, and the coin came down heads, and that professional salesman started to swear. And from the other salesmen sitting along the fence, you heard this ripple of laughter. This white-haired man, who couldn't seem to get a grasp of what was going on, had out-maneuvered and out-witted this professional salesman.

The cattle were purchased. As we were walking away, the man who sold them to Dad swore one more time and said, "Don't bother coming back," which bothered me. As we were walking back to our car, I said something to my Dad, who just laughed. He said, "Oh, he'll get over that. All that means is that we didn't pay too much for them." The cattle he bought were delivered to the farm the next day by a trucker that was headed in our direction.

In the following years, Dad stopped buying feeder cattle to grow and fatten. We just raised our own and sold them locally.

When I was twenty and farming with my Dad, who was seventy-five then, I decided to expand the operation and bought my first truck. I hauled a load of the cattle we had raised to South St. Paul. I wanted to go through the experience of dealing in the big stockyards. It was a hundred-mile trip and we had to load our cattle about four in the morning before I could start on my journey. To me, at that time, it was a very big deal.

Arriving in South St. Paul, I remember the scene as I got near the stockyards. The place I unloaded our cattle was near the big packing companies. I was overwhelmed to see thousands of people walking towards the company gates to begin their day's work, each man carrying his black, metal dinner bucket and thermos.

There was a lineup of trucks for me to follow. I had to back up quickly at an unloading dock where maybe twenty trucks were unloading at once. I was new at truck driving and most of the others were professionals. Following the stockyard procedure, I backed into a loading chute, and then jumped out of my truck and got our cattle unloaded. There were men there to help. As soon as I backed in they yelled, "Who gets 'em?" I had to fill out a ticket with our name on it, saying which commission company would be selling the cattle. Before I left home, Dad and I had picked out the name of one of the commission firms that would deal in smaller numbers of cattle. After the cattle were unloaded, I drove away to wait for about an hour until the cattle arrived at the pen where they were supposed to be. There were one hundred and twenty-five different commission companies with thousands of pens.

There were many little restaurants around the stockyards. I had time to go for breakfast before checking on our cattle that were now getting penned up and ready for sale. Those restaurants were an experience to be in. They were filled with people wearing cowboy hats, people whose boots were caked in manure. Over his shoulder, each man had a whip for driving and sorting cattle. Profanity was the language of the day. It was a total workingman's world. The delicious breakfasts were very reasonably priced. Meals were hearty because it was a place for people who worked hard, walking through those pens all day long.

After breakfast, I headed back to the walkway that went over the top of those thousands of pens. It was an experience to travel on that walkway, because down below there were all these cattle being moved, hundreds of people and thousands of cattle, all trying to find their destinations. Owners and buyers and onlookers were all walking along that overhead walkway. Some of the people down below were calling up to men they knew, some even negotiating. An owner on the walkway told a commission man in charge of selling his cattle what he expected to get. The salesman, in a very diplomatic way, replied that they may not sell that high. The market changed daily, and sometimes hourly. The commission salesmen knew the markets and often the owners weren't current.

For a twenty year old, in charge of selling cattle for the first time and alone in this big world, it was both frightening and exciting. I felt so inadequate as I talked to the people selling my cattle. Handlers were very professional and pointed out the imperfections in my cattle, and gave me tips on what the packer buyers would be looking for. As I drove my truck home that late afternoon, I knew my farm world had expanded a lot.

Over the years I continued to truck cattle to the South St. Paul Stockyards. After years, I came to know the rhythm of the stockyards. I'd like to share some of my experiences with you.

On one occasion, I had unloaded my own cattle and was walking on that overhead walkway, now very familiar with all the activity about me. I would occasionally hear people call my name and ask me what I was looking for, meaning that they had some cattle I might be interested in. Many of the buyers and sellers knew that I had brought a load of slaughter cattle up, and that I would want to take a load of feeder cattle back to the farm.

A loudspeaker was always blaring in the stockyards, calling for people to get to a phone and contact their office. I was also beginning to understand how, when crippled or sick cattle needed to be moved, there was also an outlet for them. I could still hear the sounds. "George Wier. George Wier. Call the operator." George Wier was a swarthy, slightly-built man who always seemed to be darting around looking into pens. He was the buyer of last resort. I found that his only requirement was that the cattle could walk onto his truck, or could maybe be dragged, because he had an outlet somewhere that no one questioned. Unlike many who worked there, he never seemed to be standing around visiting with friends. He was always darting about by himself. By inquiring, I found that he was a multimillionaire at a time when a million dollars was a huge amount of money, but he was in a business that few understood or inquired about.

Still on the walkway, I progressed down towards the south end of the alleys where the dealers that sell back to the farmers were located. This was the same place that I had visited with my Dad years before. When I first started dealing with these men, I was in my twenties, but looked much younger. They knew how to ridicule and intimidate a young person. If I was bidding below their asking price, they would say things like, "Sonny, why don't you go home and bring Daddy up." Very quickly, they found out that I had a truck that needed filling, and we got more serious. I found myself starting to play a game, sorta' like my Dad did years earlier.

There were certain people that I would deal with, but I was always expanding that number, and I learned that these dealers were very competitive with each other. I want to give you an example of one experience.

Because earlier I had bought cattle that turned out to be sick when I got them home, I was getting pretty cautious of a large Irishman whose every second word was a swear word. A real character, this man whose name was Carroll, though everyone called him "Bubbles," showed me his cattle. While other groups of potential buyers watched our negotiations, Bubbles told me, "Look how healthy they are, all standing there eating." I had brought a thermometer with me, and when he wasn't watching, I checked the temperature of a few cattle.

As Bubbles made his final sales pitch in front of these other people, I said, "For real healthy cattle, they are running pretty high temperatures." Bubbles just turned and walked away, and then hollered back to me, "Hey, Kid, c'mere." I thought he was impressed and would probably lower his asking price. When I got down to where he was, he said, "Get the hell out of here. We don't need you around here." I was shocked and embarrassed. And I walked back and I had to go past those same people, they were smiling, knowing something was happening. From a distance, Bubbles hollered, "Hey, Kid, get the hell out 'a here, and take your f------ thermometer with you." That produced great laughter from the onlookers, and I walked away, totally humiliated.

I learned this was just part of the game. Each dealer had his own way. I never brought a thermometer back with me again. I had broken an unwritten law, and he straightened me out. I find it interesting that over the years I bought many cattle from him, and we actually became good friends. He had just pointed out his boundaries.

A few months later, the day that I took a load of cattle to the stockyards was a Holy Day of Obligation for Catholics. This means that we were bound to attend church like we would on Sunday. It was quite an experience being in that church in St. Paul, because there were truckers like myself, and professional people, and all other types there. I saw many people from the stockyards, but my biggest shock was watching "Bubbles" come down from communion.

I found these people very interesting, almost all of them self-made men. They rose and fell with the markets, some millionaires and some bankrupt. But they were all people who lived by their wits, and as I got to know them over the years I found them challenging. In spite of our differences, I liked them and we developed a mutual respect.

I would like to tell you a story about another dealer. His name was Jack Levine. He was a very short man with a tall, stovepipe cowboy hat and a booming voice. I never managed to buy many cattle from him, but I enjoyed talking with him, and he always seemed to be there. In the later years, I heard that he had developed cancer.

On a miserable, cold, rainy, fall day, I was at the stockyards buying cattle. There, in the corner of a pen, was Jack Levine with a raincoat on. His booming voice was gone, and with just a whisper, he said, "Let me show you some cattle." They were nice looking cattle, and there were just a few, but as usual, his price was pretty high for me. So we walked back and he took up his post by the fence in the corner. I said to him, "They tell me you are worth millions. Why are you standing out here in this weather?" I will never forget the answer. With a raspy voice, barely above a whisper, he said, "That may be true, Kid. I may be worth that, but I didn't get there by selling cattle too cheap to guys like you." I said good-bye and walked away. And then I heard the cattle coming behind me. He'd opened the gate to let them go to the scales, at my price. Jack wasn't following them; he was walking in the other direction, a lonely little figure walking away in the rain. I thought of running after him and thanking him, but I didn't. I never saw Jack again. I heard later, that was his last day in the yards and that he had died soon after. I always regretted not thanking him for what he had taught me.

When I look back, those years were some of the best

years I had in the cattle business. I was not my Dad. I couldn't deal the way he dealt. I had to find my own way.

Sometimes now, driving up towards the Cities, I drive by the South St. Paul Stockyards. The pens are mostly gone. There are office buildings, hotels and a little museum in the neighborhood. The museum tries to tell, in a few items and pictures, the hundred and fifty year history of this terminal stockyard, the story of the time in history when people, the ranchers and farmers, shipped their livestock to a gathering place where they could get a reasonably fair price.

I'm really happy to have had almost twenty years of being a part of that drama. The world that seemed so large to me is no longer there, and to see what remains of it now always fills me with a little sadness.

Wounded

I think in all of our lives, there come dark times when we don't think we can go on.

This is the story of one of those times.

My wife of twenty-two years had just left and filed for divorce. The crop harvest was late. The snow came early. I had four children still at home. One night, after I picked up my daughter Mary from play practice and everyone had gone to bed, I went back out into the field to harvest two truckloads of corn so they would be ready to fill the corn dryer the next morning.

The corn head on my combine harvests six rows of corn at a time. It has lots of gathering chains that are running fast and pulling the complete corn plant into the combine. The corn head is six rows of spinning rollers and everything is open on top with fast moving chains. It spins the corn stalks through, but the ear is thrown clear and is taken by a large auger into the combine itself to be shelled. There are several lights beaming down on it, and the reflection of all those silver parts flashing makes it look like the whole front of the machine is alive. The ground was covered with snow that night, and there was snow on the corn stalks, seeming to accentuate the irreversible danger of it all.

It was a cold and lonely place, at best. I was very aware that if I would get hurt or disabled, no one would know until morning. As I was driving back and forth in the field harvesting corn, my lights picked up the reflection of the eyes of a deer. When I came near him, he seemed confused by the lights.

When he started moving along beside the machine, I realized one of his front legs was shattered at the knee. Even in the poor light, I could see the blood spraying from his wound. He was a magnificent animal, with a large rack of horns that just fit between the corn rows. Even with his woundedness, he had a majesty about him. As the combine got closer to him, he seemed confused by the lights. I stopped the forward motion of the machine. I thought that would give him a chance to move away in the darkness.

Instead, in a panic, he tried to leap over the corn head. The wounded leg threw him off balance, and instead of clearing the fifteen foot wide machine, he fell into the still-operating rollers. When I saw him falling, I found the electric shutoff switch, and the corn head stopped instantly. Even one second later would have been too late. Because everything was extremely slippery and sharp, the buck lay helpless with his legs down between the rollers.

I got out of the cab and crawled down there with him.

We began a struggle, compounded by his fear and the snow covered, slippery metal. Those flashing sharp hooves and antlers were swinging about, but mostly I remember his terror-filled eyes in the glowing light.

I felt so bad for him, and at the same time I identified with him. He was so powerful and capable, and the fact that he had survived a long time was verified by his rack of horns. A high-powered rifle bullet had shattered his knee, making him helpless and vulnerable. Most of all, he was so confused because nothing that had worked for him before would work for him now.

The high-powered bullet that had wounded me was called divorce, and like that deer I was confused. I was learning how to be a single parent and answering all those forces and demands from lawyers in distant places.

The future really looked bleak for both of us.

His blood was everywhere—on the machine and both of us. His blood, my tears, and the thrashing of his hooves against slippery metal made it a traumatic experience. Somehow, I got him rolled out of the machine and he slowly limped into the darkness.

I couldn't get the experience out of my mind. When the pressure of harvest was over, I wrote this poem. Somehow in the writing, I found some peace. Because of the pain it brings back, the poem has lain dormant for many years. I'd like to share it with you now.

Wounded

The lights reflected in his eyes
As he stood dark against the snow.
A great rack of antlers
Filled the whole corn row.

He stood so proud and mighty.
I saw the snow turn red.
He faltered when he turned to run,
As from the knee he bled.

The lights of the combine confused him.
His eyes were stark with fear.
The combine bore down on him.
This once proud, wounded deer.

As the machine was passing near him,
He gave a mighty leap.
His instinct destroyed by the bullet
That left him bleeding on the snow.

The leap would bring him to safety,
But fell far short of the mark.
He landed in the corn machine.
I found the safety switch in the dark.

The deer lay helpless on the corn head,
Bathed in the glowing light,
As man and steel, deer and snow,
Came together on that night.

With his hooves and antlers flailing,
I tried to set him free.
Warm blood on my face and hands,
Spraying from the shattered knee.

At last the deer rolled to the ground.
He limped into the dark.
Tears came while I watched him go,
Once strong, now so fragile.

We were alike, we two.

My children all asleep at home,
Sad and afraid with no mom,
Snow on the ground, harvest to do,
Cold, late, and so alone.

The buck was brought low by a bullet.
For me the shot was divorce.
Brought together that night long ago,
When I thought of him as a brother.

The deer's fate,
To be pulled down by dogs.
Mine,
To live,
Wounded.

My Finest Hour

A few years ago, I had the privilege of working with a group of people of all ages who were terminally ill, most of them suffering from AIDS or the HIV virus. It was an overwhelming experience for me, but one person in particular was so memorable. She was a young mother who looked like the picture of health, but knew she was going to die; and, she told me, would probably never see her daughters graduate or get married. She said how she wanted to live the rest of her life, what was left of it, never compromising with the truth, no matter what the price.

She hadn't shared her story in the group session, but afterwards she found me sitting alone, and she told me that when she would visit a dentist and fill out the registration form acknowledging the HIV virus, she would be told that they could not take her as a patient. She would then go on to another dentist, never denying her condition until she found someone who would say, "Come in. I can help you."

After I returned home, in the days and months that followed, I couldn't get her off my mind. I felt that I had met someone who had reached her finest hour. And I started wondering where my finest hour would be.

I think all of us have a finest hour. I want to share with you what I believe mine to be.

At the time of this story I had three young daughters. Our children seemed to be particularly susceptible to croup, a very dangerous disease. Somehow it closes up the air passage. It usually comes at night when the air is drier and you hear that whistling sound as the child is trying to breathe. It is accompanied by a raspy cough.

Mary, the youngest child, was about six months old. We called her Mame. She was always healthy, but one night about bedtime we noticed a raspy cough, and by eight o'clock in the evening her breathing was restricted. The nursery was across the hall from our bedroom, and we could hear her breathing getting more and more labored. It was very frightening.

About 11 o'clock that night we bundled her up and took her to the hospital. They put her in a crib with a croup tent, with oxygen and ice making a damp, breathable air.

Mame was a very shy child, and the experience of being in that hospital and in that tent where she could not have contact with us, seemed to paralyze her with fear. She did not move. She reminded me of a little wild animal so frightened when it is captured that it just lies there dormant.

After two days in the hospital, Mame's croup was gone and the tent had been removed, but she was still just lying there, not wanting to eat or to move. On Sunday evening my wife was staying with her, and she called me and asked me to come in. The staff had recommended keeping Mame until Monday. Because of the way she was acting, they thought she might have spinal meningitis and they wanted to do tests on her. Spinal meningitis is a horrible disease. My wife had been a nurse and knew the terrible fear around it. She was crying and wanted me to take over for the evening. So, I went up to the hospital to spend the night with Mame.

Before I went to the hospital that night, I put a little colored ball in my jacket pocket. There was a little game that Mame and I played sometimes when I put her to bed. She would sit in the crib with her little fat legs spread apart, and I would roll the bright colored ball toward her so it would go between her legs. She would watch it and then get a funny little twist to her mouth, and maybe make a little squeak. Then she would hit the ball back to me. Her eyes were always very bright when she was playing that game. When I arrived at the hospital, Mame was lying in the crib not moving a bit and her head was tipped to one side. That's why the doctor thought she might have spinal meningitis.

He was supposed to come by at eleven o'clock that night and I was to talk to him. Our doctor was a young man who went to the same church we did, and we were kinda friends with him. As I was waiting and looking at Mame, all I could think of was when I was a little boy and out helping with the seeding in the spring, there were always baby jackrabbits, just old enough to hop around. Sometimes, one was small enough so that I could catch him and bring him home, and I was determined to make a pet out of one of them. Even though I would have him in a little cage with food he would like, he would never move. He would just sit there paralyzed with fear. The only way you could tell he was alive was his breathing. His stomach would move. After a few days, my parents would say, "You have to take him back, he belongs in the wild. That baby will die if you keep it here." I never succeeded in taming one.

As I looked at Mame in that crib, not moving, I saw those little rabbits again. Because her head was tipped to one side, I took that ball and rolled it toward her. About the second time I rolled it, even though she didn't move, I saw her eyes following it. So then I started rolling the ball to different parts of the crib. Her eyes followed it even though her head didn't move.

I had never dealt with sick children, but I had dealt with sick cattle and had learned to look for the slightest sign of hope. Somehow watching Mame's eyes follow that ball, I thought, "She is not sick. She is just paralyzed with fear."

The doctor came in about midnight, and by then I was convinced that there was a misdiagnosis. The doctor's name was Bill, and he looked exhausted. Because he was a friend, with a kind of a rush of emotion, I said, "I don't think she is sick. I think she is just frightened." I said, "I feel like taking her home."

There was a moment's hesitation as he looked at me with all the tenderness that I could imagine. I had expected him to scold me for my brashness. Instead, he said to me, "There's one thing about it. She's your baby."

I was stunned. He was telling me I was the one who had to decide. I didn't know how to respond. I finally said, "Could I get her out of here tonight?" He said again, "She's your baby."

After he left the room, I was filled with emotion. Somehow he had empowered me in a way I had never dreamed. Mame was my little girl, and like those little rabbits of my childhood, I felt I had to take her home, so she could live.

I went out to the nurse's station and announced, "If you would get me a blanket, I would like to take my baby home." Making this announcement was a little like turning on a fire alarm. Everything went into action. The nurse followed me back to the room and said, "She is scheduled for tests in the morning. She is a very sick child. She must stay here."

Somehow, I became more brave than I had ever been, and I said, "She is my child, and I want to take her home. Would you please get me a blanket?"

By now there were several people saying things like, "You will be responsible if anything happens to this child," "You are endangering her life," and other things that were frightening to me. The words of Dr. Bill kept coming to me, "Remember, she is your baby."

I had to sign some papers saying I was taking her out against the wishes of the hospital staff and I was assuming all responsibility. When I carried her out of the hospital, there were people walking behind me telling me what a mistake I was making, but something in me said, "Don't turn back."

I remember it was an early spring evening. As I drove

back to the farm, I held Mame in my arms. I was grateful that we'd gotten a car with an automatic shift. I had called my wife before I left the hospital and said I was bringing Mame home. There was a gasp, and then silence on the line.

I'll never forget the way I felt walking toward the door of our house. There was such a fear in me, and so much excitement. I remember thinking, If I am wrong I can still take her back and say, "I made a mistake."

As I walked through the door of our house, Mary twisted in my arms for the first time. She recognized home. I walked past my wife, whose eyes were round and shocked, and carried Mary up to her nursery. By now, she was moving in my arms and turning her head as she recognized her room.

I sat her in her little crib, with her little legs spread apart, and I rolled that ball toward her. It was wonderful. I saw her watching the ball. By the second time I rolled it to her, she got that funny twist to her mouth, and with that little croaky sound she made she hit the ball back.

My wife, Gen, and I laughed and cried and didn't sleep much that night. Mame was home and she was well. Her fear was over.

It was more than twenty years later, after I heard that terminally ill woman describe how she wanted to spend the rest of her life, I told the story of Mame for the first time, calling it "My Finest Hour."

Healing

Many years ago I was at a festival in Tennessee, where on Sundays sacred stories are shared. I volunteered. As I listened to the other stories, I realized how much of our lives have special meaning if told in a way that is considered sacred. I want to share with you a story that I sometimes tell to a very special audience, now that I am able to make it through the telling.

My brother, Dick, was killed on his birthday, Valentine's Day 2001, by an angry young man. It was a sudden, shocking, and awful time. Although I worked on the family farm and he became a lawyer in town, people often said that he and I were close as brothers could be, and I think we were. We never talked about being close, but we were supportive of each other. It was only in the last year or so of his life, that I sometimes would give him a hug when I saw him, and vice versa. His death was such big news that we had to go through a lot of publicity in dealing with it. One day I had the three major network television trucks sitting in my driveway, all waiting for interviews.

Spring came early in 2001, and on the farm that is a very demanding time. By April, I was still exhausted from all the trauma. I think I was still dealing with some depression and I was physically worn down. My son, Tom, and I were farming together, and he was pushing hard to finish the spring planting, knowing that is the way I would want it.

It was about eleven o'clock one night when I finally said to Tom, "I can't do anymore. I've gotta go home." As I drove to Grandma's house, where I was living then, I realized I didn't have anything to eat there. I was covered with the dust and the dirt of the day. I wanted to just forget it and go home, but I knew I should get something. So I drove out to the supermarket, hoping against hope that no one there would recognize me. I was lucky.

When I arrived, there were only a few clerks and about five customers. I walked down the aisle looking for something to make sandwiches with. As I came to the end of the aisle, I met a lady coming from the other direction. She was in a jean jacket, about forty-five years old, and looked like she had a lot of spunk, but her face showed a hard life. For just a moment she looked at me. When anyone stared at me like that I knew that they'd had some dealings with Dick and recognized me. She turned quickly away, but wherever we went, we kept bumping into each other. Finally, at the checkout counter, we met again, and she said to me, "I just have to tell you."

She began the story. She said, "I am not from here, and I

was in jail. They handed me a sheet of paper with the names of all the lawyers available for my defense." She said, "It seemed so foolish, because none of the names meant anything to me. I looked down the list, and I don't know the reason, I picked this name. After a while, a quiet man in a dark suit came to my cell. He began the questions. The first thing I noticed was that he treated me with respect. I didn't respect myself; I didn't know how he could respect me. So I had to tell him, 'I don't know that I will ever be able to pay you.' But he didn't answer. After he finished his interview, he posted bail for me, and I was free to leave until the trial."

"At the hearing, the verdict allowed me to leave. I was free to go. I said to him again, 'I don't know that I will ever be able to pay you.' He looked at me very directly. He said, 'You don't belong here. You can do a lot better than this. You go and turn your life around, and don't ever come back here, and that will be my pay.'"

Then she said, "My life is totally different now. I am not the same person I was then." By now, we were holding each other's hands and we were both crying. She looked at me so vulnerably with those teary eyes, and said, "I just had to tell you."

We parted then, and I think we both knew that we would never see each other again.

In the days and weeks that followed, I kept thinking of that night, and something became clear to me that I guess I had always known. Whatever my brother had accumulated in his estate was left behind, but she helped me to understand that how he affected other people, and how they felt about him. He got to take that with him.

Letting go of him was very hard, but that most random meeting in the grocery store, when I felt so completely vulnerable, that was the story I clung to.

Photo by Tom Cotter

This is the tractor the killdeer challenged to save her nest.

Photo by Tom Cotter

Two calves that are only a week old find a pal.

Photo by Paulette Mertes

You can't beat a good audience.

Photo provided by Cotter family

Michael brings Minnesota farm stories to an Ohio festival.

Photo by International Storytelling Center

Michael enjoys his weeklong storytelling residencies at the International Storytelling Center in Jonesborough, Tennessee.

Photo by Tom Cotter

In 1929 when this barn was built, all of the power was provided by horses. Today, the tractor, disc and ripper are a small portion of the equipment needed to run the farm.

Photo by Tom Cotter

The combine kicks up a cloud of dust as it harvests twelve rows of soybeans.

Photo by Tom Cotter

This donkey was purchased to protect new born calves from the coyotes. Michael's granddaughter Vanessa Cotter welcomed him to the family picnic.

Photo by Tom Cotter

Julian Sanchez, Michael's great-grandson, LOVES big tractors.

Photo by Tom Cotter

Young calves enjoy the end of summer.

Photo by Bev Jackson Cotter

Michael is waiting for students to arrive at the Young Authors/Young Artists Conference in Mankato, Minnesota.

Photo by Bev Jackson Cotter

Michael received a warm welcome in Mount Ayr, Iowa.

Photo by Bev Jackson Cotter

Michael's audience responds to an earthy story at Living History Farms in Des Moines, Iowa.

Photo by Tom Cotter

A good farmer starts his day early in the spring.

Photo by Tom Cotter

A barn warmed by livestock is a pleasant place to be on a winter day in Minnesota.

Photo by Agnes Boss

Michael and Bev Cotter strike a pose in the spirit of Grant Wood's
American Gothic

The Best Man

My mother always brought a little bit about religion into each day. Around her, it was not safe to say that you were having a bad day. If you did, you would hear her admonishing tone, telling you that God might give you a worse day for complaining without good reason.

I think of that as I start telling this story, because on a hot July Saturday afternoon I thought that I was having a bad day.

I had driven out to the farm center located about three and a half miles south of Austin. It's a place that sells agricultural supplies, and I was going to pick up some chemical to spray on weeds. I had my afternoon planned, and it was with some frustration that I found the place closed. During the busy season they are open every day, and I hadn't remembered that in the slower seasons they closed at noon on Saturdays.

It was a muggy, ninety degree day without a breath of air, and I was sitting in my pickup with sweat on my back and on my forehead, wondering what to do next. Then a story happened.

From where I was parked, I could see Highway 218 south of Austin, about a half mile away. There was the usual traffic with cars and trucks, but then I saw a figure in the distance. It looked like a person on a bicycle, and it was hard to make out, but it seemed like he was wearing a top hat and a long coat. He was peddling furiously.

I forgot my problems and turned all of my attention on who that figure was and what he was about. Much to my surprise, he turned onto the road leading to the farm center and started coming towards me. I watched him come closer. He was riding one of those bikes where you lean forward over the handlebars and peddle furiously with your head down; and this is what he was doing, with some alteration. With his high top hat, he had to hold his head at a different angle. The long tails of his formal dress coat floated behind him in that hot air.

It was like some kind of dream. I wondered if I was really seeing what I was seeing. Everything about him seemed frantic as he finally rode up.

Since I was the only one sitting in the parking lot, he rode toward me, his face a color of purple you don't see very often. As he got near, I was going to ask him something, but the word, "Water" was all I heard him say. "Is there any water?" And he did look like he needed water.

I knew where there was a faucet on the outside wall in back of the building. Together we went back there and found it, and he got down on his knees and drank that water the way I remember our draft horses drinking when they'd been working all day in the sun.

It's very satisfying to give water to a man as thirsty as he was. Sweat ran down his face, and his formal coat had dark stains on it where sweat had soaked through. His cumberbund seemed to be one more place for sweat to accumulate.

Due to the condition of my old pickup, I would never just offer a ride to a man in a top hat and a formal tuxedo—or anyone who was dressed well at all—so I asked, "Can I help you?" He said that he was afraid that he would miss the wedding. He had no problem with getting in my truck.

Now, my pickup sits out in the field much of the time, and is covered with dust and dirt, inside and out. It carries months of accumulated clutter, parts, and oil from various farm problems.

We put his bike in the back amid the residue of broken parts and wrenches. That modern bike seemed out of place in the back of the truck, just like the young man in his top hat in the cab. As we drove off with a roar, 'cause the muffler had a hole in it; it didn't seem like the proper way for a man in a tuxedo to arrive at a church. The one bright spot was that he seemed so grateful. He never complained a bit.

As we rode towards Austin he was able to catch his breath enough to tell me his story. He had come from another state, I think Michigan, and was to be best man in the wedding of his best friend. He was staying at the home of the bride, about ten miles from Austin. The wedding was going to take place at three in the afternoon on Saturday. The church was all prepared, and everything was going smoothly.

Many people were gathered for an early lunch at the home of the bride, and while everyone was visiting, her father decided to go upstairs and take a little nap. With so many guests and friends there, no one noticed for awhile that he didn't return.

About three hours before the wedding was to happen, the bride discovered that her dad had died. Pandemonium broke loose in that house—frantic phone calls, father had to be sent to the mortuary, the death certificate …

Finally, it was decided they would go ahead with the wedding because people had come from so far away.

With all the turmoil, the young man now riding beside me in the pickup was so distraught that he decided to just walk out by himself for a few minutes to collect his thoughts. He was going to be the best man and he wanted to be very helpful. He said he hadn't walked very far and he had only been gone a few minutes, but when he returned to the home of the bride, he found everyone gone and the house locked.

A sort of panic seized him. Somehow they had totally forgotten him, and there were no neighbors close by. He knew the wedding was going to happen within an hour or so, and he did know where the church was. The one car sitting in the yard was locked, but in the garage he saw a ten-speed bicycle, and he thought he could probably make it in time for the wedding, if he hurried.

By the time he finished his story, I had this nervous and perplexed young man in front of the church. He jumped out of my pickup and raced toward the entrance. Glancing through the door, I saw just a few of the people in the wedding party. Everyone seemed to be frantic; the crowd was milling about, and it seemed that chaos was the order of the day. I realized that he had left his bike in my pickup, so I put it near the front of the church where they could find it later.

I don't know how the wedding went, or how the bride was able to handle the joy of a wedding and the sorrow of her father's death on the same day. I don't imagine the young man will ever forget the time he came to Minnesota to be the best man at his friend's wedding.

I had gotten so involved with his problem, I had totally forgotten mine. God didn't give me a bad day. He just showed me what one could really be like.

The Bronco

When I was a young boy on that Minnesota farm, we had many large draft horses, and they were an important part of our lives. They provided the power for most of the field work, and occasionally we rode them.

Their backs were broad, they had large hooves, and most of them stood very tall. Sitting on the back of one of those large work horses my feet would stick straight out, and I only had that thick, heavy mane to hang on to. These horses were for work, but I dreamed of a horse just to ride.

I didn't know enough to ask for any particular breed, like an Appaloosa or a Quarter Horse. I just wanted a riding horse, and I knew exactly what he would look like and what his name would be.

In our newspaper, in the funnies, there was a comic strip named "Red Rider." I don't know why they called it a funny paper, 'cause it was never funny at all. Red Rider was a lean, red-haired cowboy trying to do a little good in his part of the world. His companion was an Indian boy named Little Beaver.

I didn't think that Red Rider was the most important part of that comic strip. It was his horse that I loved. The horse was a tall, graceful, black horse with three white stockings and a long black mane. His long black tail always seemed to be blowing majestically in the wind, while he stood gracefully, figuring out how to help Red Rider out of his latest problem.

I thought that horse was perfectly beautiful. And to cap that beauty, he had a white star on his forehead. I knew that someday I'd have a horse that would look like him, and I would name him "Thunder"—just like Red Rider's horse.

I did what all kids do. I begged and begged. And finally my father, in an uncharacteristic move, agreed to get me a horse, but I would have to wait for the right one. The right one meant it would be a good horse, but it would be cheap.

After a seemingly endless period of time, one day he said, "Let's go look at your horse." There had been a notice in the paper that carloads of broncos would be arriving in Austin, so on a Sunday afternoon we went to the rail yard. Now, if you drive by Austin on Interstate 90 where the new Hormel plant is, back in the early forties that area was just a pasture. East of that, where the industrial park is now, there was a rail yard. All sorts of animals: cattle, sheep, and goats were brought in from the western states in livestock cars and then were unloaded in those large pens. It was a common sight to see them grazing in that pasture in front of the Hormel plant, where they waited for their time to be slaughtered.

On this Sunday, in those railroad pens with the high boards and the railroad tie posts, my dad and I went looking for my horse. I was not prepared for the sight that greeted me.

At one end of the pen, the local people who were interested in the horses were standing. In the center of the pen were two cowboys, tall and lean, with dusty clothes and faces the color of the fence itself.

What caught my attention most were the horses they were sitting on. I had only seen our big draft horses, sleek and grain fed, muscular and healthy. These horses were like skeletons, tiny and thin, their manes and tails missing. There were only scabs where their manes had been. I learned that the other horses had eaten the manes away. Their tails were just stumps with no hair. All the long hair was gone.

The cowboys looked a lot like their horses. They weren't the "real" cowboys like we know today, like the late John Wayne and President Reagan. These were the dusty old-fashioned kind. There was a cowboy with a home-rolled cigarette hanging from his mouth. The cigarette was fat in the center and twisted on the ends. His horse's head hung down, and its neck without a mane didn't arch beautifully. It kind of had a bow in it, and the horse's ears didn't stand up straight. They sort of tipped out. That horse looked like he was just too tired, or too old, to stand straight.

At the far end of the pen was a whole bunch of little broncos, thin and pitiful and wild. They, too, had no manes or tails, and as they tried to crawl over each other they got tighter and tighter into the corner. Their eyes had a wild look, with a white ring around the edge as they struggled to get into the farthest corner. They reminded me of a pile of maggots moving up and down and going over.

If you wanted to buy a horse, you gave the cowboy twenty-five dollars. Then, he reached into the gunnysack hanging from the saddle horn and pulled out a new white lariat rope, unfurled the rope, and touched his spurs to his horse. His horse, too, had those wild eyes. You pointed to the horse you wanted in the pile, and the loop sailed out. Out of that pile of struggling horse flesh came a little bronco, spinning and twisting in the air, squealing and rolling on the ground. Then the cowboy handed you the rope, and you got the rope and the horse for twenty-five dollars.

My dad was an old-timer, and when he saw the situation, these horses wild and untrained with the rope, he had a change of heart.

Whenever he wanted to intimidate someone, Dad called him, "Shorty," no matter how tall he was. He went up to this cowboy that looked so tall, and he said, "Shorty, what'll you take for that horse you are riding?" Seventy-five dollars later, the cowboy stripped the saddle from his own horse, and I got on up on its back.

That horse's back was sharp as a narrow board, and there was no mane to hang on to. A friend of my dad had opened its mouth, and after checking its teeth, announced, "He's just comin' three." He was a young bronco.

As I rode him out of that pen that evening, we passed several of those other young broncos lying in the dirt. They just would not give in to that rope, and they had broken their necks.

My horse was broke, and you knew he was broke because he had spur marks on his side, just scabbing over. He'd had one rough encounter with a cowboy, and like the other horses, when he looked at you he had those wild eyes. It was a long trip home.

This horse was a long ways from my dream. When I let him walk, his head hung down and he sort of plodded, but if my heels touched the spur marks, he went up in the air like a wild animal. When we got near our farm, my brother came out to meet me. I think he was jealous that I was getting a horse, but when he saw us, he just laughed. And that made me mad.

At first, my horse would not eat the hay and the grain that our big draft horses ate. He didn't seem to know what they were. He would just eat the weeds along the fence and the old bedding in the horse stall.

Very shortly he began to eat that grain, and he was crazy for it. The energy that hit that young bronco was unbelievable. About a week later, my brother rode him out one morning, and the horse came home without him. When I saw Dick walking, I didn't even feel bad.

It was then I noticed how my horse was changing. His head had come up and his neck was arched. This young bronco was coming of age.

In a few weeks he grew a long black mane and a long black tail, and he became the deepest chestnut I'd ever seen. He stood majestically, and for the first time I realized he had three white stockings and a white star on his forehead. And I named him "Thunder," and he ran like the very wind itself. And I never had another. I loved him like only a twelve year old could love a horse, but it was a one-sided love affair.

I think his beginnings had been too harsh, or the cowboys had been too rough. He wasn't mean, but if I ever let go of the reins, or if he was able to jerk them out of my hands, he ran away—except for one time. Here's my story.

It takes place a few years later, when I was about sixteen. We had a herd of stock cows on our farm. My dad called them western cows. They were mostly Hereford breed and they spent their summers on a distant pasture, where they had their young. In the winter they were fed among the sheds on the farm.

One of them was going to have its baby calf out of season, and one of the characteristics of a stock cow is to go off by itself to have its young. On a bitterly cold January Sunday, this cow got away from the herd, and we knew she had gone to have her calf. To search for her, I rode my bronco through the snow drifts to the far corners of the farm. I found her where Interstate 90 now runs. Then, it was a marshy area with tall grasses and brush growing. The calf had already been born. The cow had cleaned him off and he was lying in that tall grass, with the snow drifting around him. His ears were already frozen in the bitter cold. She had done everything she could, and she was standing over him as I rode up.

It looked like some famous painting, the cow standing there quietly, both of them waiting for the inevitable. I got down off my horse into that deep crusted snow and tried to pick up the calf. Even though he was half frozen, he was slippery and heavy and awkward. Plus, my horse was nervous and jerking on the reins.

I turned to that horse and I said, "You've gotta stand," and I let go of the reins and I picked up the calf. When I turned around I expected the horse would be gone.

I don't know if it was the wind, or the desperation in my voice, or just the way things are, but I will never forget the scene as that wild-eyed horse danced around me. His neck was arched and his ears were pointed. His nostrils were flared wide as he snorted, sounding almost like a train whistle in the distance. He danced around me, but he didn't run. And eventually, he let me lay that newborn calf across his back. He stood long enough so I could get up behind the calf, and we started for home with the cow following.

Later in the warm barn, his frozen ears dropped off, but the calf lived. And I never let go of the horse's reins again, but what he ran.

Many years later, I was asked to do a program in a nursing home in Rochester, Minnesota. It was St. Patrick's Day, and I was excited, being quite new as a storyteller.

People were being wheeled into this big recreation room. Some were coming in and sitting in chairs. As I was talking to the people in charge, there was a lot of excitement in the air. Some of the residents were hard of hearing, and talked loudly to each other during the program. Sometimes, right in the middle of my story, they would say, "I can't hear him. Can you?"

For the most part, things seemed to be going quite well—except for one little man who was sitting almost directly in front of me.

I didn't know why they had brought him; he looked so pitiful. He sat in a wheelchair and his frail, little body was supported entirely by straps. His head would have been right down on his knees, had not that strap held him back. His arms hung down by the side of the wheelchair, and he seemed totally "out of it."

I told my stories and tried not to look at him, because there was no response from him. The program ended and it seemed to have gone quite well. As the aides were coming to wheel the people away, I wanted to talk to one of the directors. On my way past this man, I almost missed seeing his hand down near the wheel of his wheelchair. That hand was fluttering. It was the first movement I'd seen from him. Because his head was near his lap, I had to get down on my knees in front of him to see his face.

It was the first time I'd seen his eyes. They were not "out of it," as I had imagined. They were very bright and were rolled way up as he was trying to see me. When he spoke, his voice was only a raspy whisper, but I'll never forget it. He said, "One time … my dad … brought two carloads of broncos … and I helped him."

Then his body relaxed, he sagged back into his straps,

and his head dropped down closer to his lap. I tried to respond, saying, "Two carloads of broncos! They are wild!" But he had finished, and the nurse came and wheeled him away.

As I drove home that day, I thought of that man, helpless and pitiful, but he knew if he could tell me that he had handled broncos that I would know he had once been powerful.

He needed to tell me his story, and I had almost missed it.

The Balky Horse

When I was a young boy, one of the people that drifted onto our farm to work was a man named John. He had white hair and I thought of him as an old man, strong built and very quiet. On summer nights the hoboes gathered under the windmill. With the sound of water pumping into the tank, they told their stories. John was born in the late 1800s and one night something triggered this story.

He told of when he was a teenager, and how they lived on a farm in northeast Iowa for a time, where the farms were small and the land was hilly. John went to a country school there, with a few neighbors and his family. John, like others, grew up shy and socially awkward, especially around the opposite sex. Oftentimes, brothers and sisters of that time continued to run the farm, and were never married. At about sixteen, John was, I'm sure, a strong built young man.

Oftentimes on Sunday mornings, a neighbor who lived a couple of miles away, a woman and her teenage daughter, would drive by with a horse and buggy on their way to church.

John was fascinated by the young woman, and this normally very quiet man described the young girl sitting up beside her mother as "slender as a willow, and she always wore a white dress."

John found out that her name was Wilda, and on Sunday mornings he would wait for her to pass, hiding behind a tree or in a building so she wouldn't see him. It seemed that this was a story that would have no fulfillment, but one Sunday morning John had a stroke of luck.

The horse that Wilda's mom was driving balked right in front of their driveway. Now, a balking horse is one that stops and will not move. You can hit them, or do anything you want, but they will not move. When I tell these stories in cities, where people don't know anything about horses, I have to compare them to teenagers so they will understand.

Now John saw opportunity, and he was a man of action. He didn't know much about women, but he knew a lot about balky horses. He grabbed an armful of hay and raced down the driveway, and threw it under the horse. I think from all time, men have tried to impress women, and John was going to impress these women as he lit a match and threw it into the hay. As that flame came up under the horse, he quit balking. He gave one leap ahead and stopped again. You know where the fire was now? It was under the buggy.

I still remember John that night. He was no longer under the windmill; he was at the end of that driveway. As the flames caught on the floor of the buggy, he said, "By God. Then

I had something."

But he was a strong young man, and he grabbed the wheels of the buggy and tipped it up on its side and tried to brush the flames off the floor where it was burning. It was just too much for one man, even one like John. The buggy got away from him and rolled into the ditch, along with Wilda and her mom and Wilda's white dress.

The story ended there, and that's the way stories are. They sometimes bring back memories that you don't want to remember. But then there's the audience, and one of the other men said, "John, whatever happened to Wilda?"

John was quiet. A sad look came over his face, and he said, "I don't know. By God, I don't know." He said, "Those people started driving another way to church.

"The stories from our lives make us who we are. That story, above all others, is the one that seems to draw a response.

I was in a senior center in western Minnesota, and after telling that story, a white haired man came up to me with a big smile. He said, "Your story brought back such memories," and he immediately launched into his story.

He told me that when he was about fourteen years old, he lived on a big dairy farm. He said his father was a big, strong German man who was very proud of his operation, and also very quiet. But once a year, on Sunday morning in their little church, the pastor would stand up and mention that, once again, the ten acre field that the church was set on was planted in hay; that Mr. Schmidt had again rented that hay field, and not only did he give a generous donation, but they always knew the field would be mowed timely and it would always be neat. He said how his dad just sat with his arm across the back of the seat, and was just so proud.

The day came to gather up the hay on the church property. "My brother and I were out there early in the morning, 'cause the circus was coming to town that afternoon. We knew if we didn't have that hay finished, we wouldn't get to the circus. We were pitching the hay up on the wagon and had about a half a load on, when one of the horses in our team balked, and would not move."

"I was older than my brother, and maybe because he said, 'What are we going to do? We won't get to the circus,' I felt I had to do something. So I kicked some hay under the horse and lit it on fire. It was the same as in your story. The horses moved ahead and stopped again. Now my brother and I were under the wagon, frantically trying to get the burning hay out from under it. We were getting burned, but we could not stop the fire, and it got into the load of hay."

He gave an imitation of the horses as they smelled the smoke. Horses have bridles that have blinders on them so they can only see what is in front of them, and he imitated how both horses turned their necks way around to look back. When they saw the fire, they took off running. He said, "With the wagon rolling across the field, it became like a torch. The horses were running faster and faster, shaking the burning hay off the wagon and spreading the fire wherever they went."

"Because the church property was well fenced, they were having a hard time getting out of the hay field. Finally, they broke through the fence, tore the wagon loose and they were free."

The man in front of me became quiet. His smile was gone as the memories came back. He said, "I don't know if the circus came to town that day or not. The whole town had to turn out to help save the church. My Dad was so angry," he said, "I was not allowed to speak at the table at all. It was like I was not even there. He had been so humiliated."

"Day after day and week after week, I had to be silent at the table. I couldn't take it. One day I just walked away, and I never came back."

By now tears were streaming down his face. I reached out to him, but he moved away. I wanted to say, "How awful it must have been," but he was leaving. His last words to me were, "I don't know why your story brought it all back."

I was speaking at a small museum honoring the history of Mennonites, known as Germans from Russia. As I finished speaking and was walking with my hosts toward the table where they were serving their unique foods, an older couple blocked my path. I don't know if it was a brother and sister or a husband and wife. He was unshaven, very shy looking, and was wearing bib overalls. She was quite a round lady, with hair that was poorly cut and a dress that was out of style, and looked like it might have fit her better several years earlier. She had him by the arm and was pulling him along. He was so shy, he didn't want to stand and talk to me. I noticed he had a little tobacco juice running down the corners of his mouth, and I thought of what my Irish Dad used to say. Dad was a little prejudiced. He said, "That's the sign of a level-headed Norwegian."

The woman said, "So you're a storyteller." And I said, "Yes." She was kind of pulling the man towards me, but he didn't say anything. My hosts were waiting and I was trying to move on. Then she gave him a good jerk, right in front of me, and said, "Tell him your story." It was amazing. This terribly shy man with his head down, looking helpless, all of a sudden straightened up like he had purpose. He was on a mission.

He said, "My Dad was from the Old Country." And I gather from what he said, a Mennonite man was the total authority in the family at that time. On Mennonite farms, the buildings were clustered close together.

One day, when the boy was about twelve, he said his Dad was driving a horse and wagonload of corn up a hill, where he was going to leave it for the hogs near their shelter. The man said that horse was his friend, but the ground was muddy and the load was too heavy for it, so the horse decided to quit pulling. It balked. The Mennonite father was angry. He told this twelve year old boy to go to the house, that he was to get the whip called the "black snake" from their driving buggy. The fear of the twelve year old was reflected in the man's face as he said, "I don't know how I had the strength to stay there and disobey my father." After his Dad left to get the whip himself, the boy picked up the reins and called to that horse to "Pull!" He described that horse, when he heard the voice of his friend, and how it turned its head way around so it could see him.

He didn't know if it was his frantic voice, or that the horse believed in him, but he said, "That horse started to pull, and he had to almost lie down to move that load. He pulled the load of corn up the hill, and I unhitched him and took him to the barn where he would be safe. Then I hid."

His father came back with the whip and he called to the boy. As he told me the story, I could see the fear in his face. "My father said, 'Where is the horse?' And I said, 'He is in his stall in the barn.' It was then my Dad noticed that the wagon was right where he wanted it."

"He swore, in German, and—carrying his whip—he walked back towards his buggy." The story ended.

I'll never forget that the man was standing straight, powerful and with purpose. At his side, the woman was standing silent. Then they both realized where they were, and he assumed that same awkward, shy pose. She took his arm and they walked away. I never caught up with my host couple, but as I drove the one hundred and twenty miles home that day, I realized that I had heard the most important story of that day.

Out of the Fog

When my family was very young and numbered only three children, we made a significant trip over Christmas. Normally, we would stay at home with work and livestock keeping us there, but this year we went to Montana to be with my wife's family through Christmas and New Year's.

We drove our car to their home in western Montana. To take care of my guilt for being away from the work on the farm, I flew to Oregon to visit my aunt, who owned farmland that I rented. That way, I combined a family and business trip.

Aunt Mabel was quite elderly and was the only heir of Uncle Mart's estate. He was my Dad's only brother, and I had last seen my aunt at my uncle's funeral. She was a good businesswoman, wanting the rent paid on time, but she was not wanting to know about any problems with the land.

She and a young nephew met me at the plane in Pendleton, Oregon, and then drove me through a foggy sixty miles to her home. I planned to stay three days, and then return to Bozeman for New Year's Eve with my wife's family.

While visiting with her I noticed she had become very forgetful. I would give her the house key, and then she would forget and think I still had it. She talked a lot about who she wanted to have her things when she was no longer here.

She loved to show me the prized dishes that sat in her cupboard. She was Spanish, and with flashing eyes said that some of the dishes had come by sailing ship around the Cape. She prized them highly, and carefully handed them to me to look at. Then she would tell me, "Now, you're not getting this. It is for 'so and so.'" It was her kind of humor. As I looked at those rare dishes, I was very nervous. I saw that they had cracks in them, and I knew if one broke she would never forgive me. I wanted them to get back in her cupboard without any damage.

Of course, I was interested in buying the land that had been greatly improved over the years, although she didn't really know anything about it. She dismissed my questions, simply saying, "Uncle Mart took care of that," and refused to talk about it.

My business with her was soon complete and I was anxious to get back to the plane. Aunt Mabel liked company, and said, "This is the season of black ice and fog, and your plane won't fly." She seemed right. Each day was foggier than the last, and I was getting nervous. I finally made an appointment with the nephew to take me to the airport, whether the plane flew or not.

The last day I was at Aunt Mabel's I went out in their old barn. Uncle Mart had been a well driller, and much of his old equipment stood in the barn where it had been parked after his heart attack in the 1930s. He had planned to use it again and had sold only a little of it. But, there it was. With a little light coming through the dusty windows, I could see all the ancient, and once valuable, machinery that had allowed him to drill a thousand feet to strike water.

His last purchase, before he got sick, was a panel truck. It was the predecessor of the modern van. This had only a driver's seat, and then a bench along the side for people to sit on. From the walls of the truck hung pulleys, cables, wrenches, and other well drilling equipment of the 20s and 30s. The driver's seat was unusual. It was on a low post that came out of the floor. Uncle Mart was a tall man, and it must have been fitted just for him. The truck looked like it had been parked one night in the barn, and then had sat there for almost fifty years, patiently waiting.

As I stood among the working equipment in the old barn, I was reminded of his quiet humor and the one time he and I had joined together to tease Aunt Mabel. I had visited their home when I was seventeen. Aunt Mabel had decided to grow tomatoes and was very frustrated when the vines grew and grew, but no tomatoes came on them. Uncle Mart and I decided to play a trick on her. With green thread and a needle, we sewed tiny green apples onto the tomato plant. It was quite a job, and when I asked him how many he thought we should put on, with a very gentle, sly smile, he said he thought, "We might as well put on enough for one good meal."

The next morning I left for the airport in spite of the fog. My aunt warned me that I would be back, but I knew that it was time for me to leave. I wanted to be back in Montana before New Year's Eve, when there would be no planes flying. When I got to the airport, I thanked the nephew and said good-bye, assuring him that I would find a way and he should not wait.

I felt a great sense of freedom, but not for long. Only one plane landed, and that was going in the opposite direction. The rest of the flights passed over, not landing in the fog shrouded airport.

Being in my early thirties and very impatient, I soon found a man who was driving east a hundred miles, who would take me to another airport. This sounded like a good idea. So he and I drove foggy, winding roads only to find that planes were not leaving that airport either. When he let me off, I was in the same situation as earlier, but now it was much later in the day, very foggy and getting dark.

I managed to catch one more ride trying to reach Spokane, where I could catch a train to Montana before they stopped at midnight for the New Year's Eve holiday. The next car had taken me to a highway, and left me off in the fog near a sign that said "Spokane - 32 miles."

By now, it was totally dark and there seemed to be no cars traveling. I learned later that the main highway was a few miles away, and I had been left on the old highway. Behind me was a little town with one motel sign flashing. Three of the letters were not lit; only the "O" and the "L" flashed. The sign seemed as dreary as my life right then, and I thought I might have to spend the next two days there—if they had a room. I was dressed for flying, not standing on the side of the road in a damp, cold fog.

When a lone car would come, I would pull my light coat down from over my head, smooth my hair with my hand, and try to look extremely safe. The approaching car would turn on its bright lights to try to pick me out of the fog, and then I would hear this "whoosh" sound as the car accelerated, wanting to get by that lonely figure as quickly as possible. In less than a minute the tail lights would disappear in the fog and only the sound of the car could be heard as it drove away.

I would pull my light coat up over my head again to try to keep from shivering, as much from the hopelessness of my plight as from the dampness of the night, waiting for the next car that would follow exactly the same procedure.

After an endless amount of time, I was shaking so bad from the cold, I knew I would have to give up. It became kind of an endurance contest with myself. The cold was almost unbearable, and by this time I was shaking uncontrollably. I started to say to myself, after each car disappeared, "I'll wait for one more car." Then I'd find myself saying it again car after car, before I finally accepted the fact that I might need to walk to that motel with only two of its letters flashing. Before long, I reached the end of my patience and knew I would truly walk after only one more car.

The last car approached in the distance. This one was different, almost from the beginning. The lights seemed extra yellow, and the sound of the vehicle told me it was a very old car. When the headlights picked me out of the fog, it started slowing down.

My hopes soared. When it came up beside me and stopped, I realized it was not a car at all, but an old panel truck. The only lights were its dim headlights, and it was totally dark within.

I didn't care. I was so happy. With one hand I grabbed my suitcase from the ground, and with the other I grabbed the door handle. It was locked. The old truck was at a noisy idle, and nothing was happening. Finally the window opened, and out of that pitch black darkness came an old man's voice and the question I will never forget. "What religion are you?"

I loosened my grip on the door handle and wondered what I should answer. If this was only Utah, I'd say I was a Mormon. To get off that road, I was ready for conversion. Because I didn't know what else to do, I gave the full truth. I said, "I am a Roman Catholic," and waited for the truck to drive away. There was a moment, and then a click. The door opened.

As I climbed in, I could barely see the driver of that panel truck. I could just make out a figure on that lone seat by the dashboard that seemed to have no lights. I said, "I need to go to Spokane to a train station. " No answer. I said, "The train leaves at midnight."

The gears ground, the old truck lurched forward and I was thrown off balance. This, apparently, was an old work truck, for there was a rattle of pulleys and chains on the inside of the truck. I heard the old man's voice say, "I know," like it answered all my questions.

He went through the gears. In the darkness, I finally found my balance and a bench along the side of the truck. It seemed to make a lot of noise as it went along. I tried to engage the driver in conversation, without much success. As my eyes got used to the darkness, I could make out some of the things hanging on the side of the panels. I saw big wrenches, pulleys, and rolls of what looked like cable—all bouncing and rattling as we rolled along. My driver didn't speak, but when we would encounter a car out of the fog, for just a second, its lights would silhouette an old man sitting very low on an odd little seat, almost like an old armchair. The signs on the side of the road said we were getting near Spokane. I saw by my watch, which could illuminate, that time was gonna be awfully tight. I said again to the old man, "I need to get to the train station." The answer came back, "I know."

Eventually we were in the city, though never on lighted streets. It seemed like we were always on back streets. He was turning corners and shifting gears a lot, and he didn't have time for conversation.

It was almost midnight as we pulled up to a lighted building. Even though the fog was thick, I knew we were at the train depot. He didn't stop. He went around a corner, and pulled into a darkened area in the parking lot. There was a street light right over the depot entrance, but he didn't stop until he was in the darkness.

As I was ready to go out the door, I reached my hand out to him and said, "You've saved my life." But no hand met mine. I could just see the silhouette of that old man behind the steering wheel.

I tried to thank him again, but the door was open. As

he let out the clutch, all of a sudden, I was jerked off the step and out beside the truck. I was going to get around in front, but the gears ground and the truck was soon moving away. I could hear it in the fog, but the tail lights seemed to disappear almost immediately. Because I figured he'd have to come back through that entrance, I stood waiting under the street light. There must have been another way out of that parking lot. The panel truck never came back.

I remember that lighted depot, with hundreds of people milling around. It seemed like heaven—the warmth and light. I went up to the ticket window to buy a seat for the train to Montana. The woman said, "You are in luck. The train leaves in less than ten minutes. You're lucky you came to the right depot. The other one does not have a train running to Montana tonight." Then she added, "I understand it's a very foggy night out." I told her, "I already knew that."

The train pulled up, I got on and started that long ride back to Bozeman. Other people were sleeping and it was quiet, but I had a hard time settling down. I arrived in Montana the next morning and joined my family, and that evening, on New Year's Eve, we went to a party.

My heart wasn't really in it. I kept thinking about that old man and the old panel truck, and that mysterious ride where we never talked. He seemed to know everything I needed, and I was filled with wonder.

The Potato Story

WHERE IT ALL STARTED

In 1978 a brochure came into our home. I'm not sure how it got there. It said there was a team of professional storytellers from New York City that would be doing a weekend workshop at St. Catherine's College in St. Paul. My wife, Gen, showed it to me and said, "This looks like something you might be interested in."

I was a busy young farmer with a family, a lot of cattle, and very little time. Although the word "storytelling" caught my attention, I pretty much dismissed it. But it stayed in my mind.

I decided to drive the hundred miles to the St. Paul workshop with the thought, "If it's not interesting I'll come back home." The team of presenters was from New York City, and that was intimidating to me, so I just dismissed them thinking they would be odd and I would not understand them.

The opening evening event pretty much confirmed my fears. People told fairy tales, folk tales, stories from other cultures, and stories from history. For the most part, they were pretty theatrical. There was a Jewish rabbi who was a real character, I thought. It was interesting, but I got to thinking I should leave after the morning session. I had more important things to do. But because lunch was included in the program, I decided to stay for the meal.

I sat at a table with a couple of strangers, and eventually it was just this forty-something year old woman and myself. Later, walking towards my car, I realized that even though we were strangers, we'd had the most unusual conversation. It was like we had known each other for a long time, and yet we had nothing in common.

Before I headed home I decided to check on the afternoon workshops. To my surprise, the woman I'd eaten lunch with was on stage describing her session. I was shocked. I didn't know that she was one of the presenters, so I decided to go to her workshop. Her name was Gioia Timpanelli, and she talked about the "personal story." She had us sit in a circle. Everyone there was a stranger to me, and there were maybe twenty-five of us. Her opening statement was, "We all are storytellers, and the story we are telling is our life. Like an artist needs to paint a picture, we need to take that out and hang it up on the wall where we, and the world, can look at our life together." Then she asked for a volunteer to be the first one in the circle to tell their story. As it almost always happens in those situations, a middle aged man led off with a slightly naughty story—a canned joke. I was very uncomfortable, and I remember her response. She listened so intently, like it was the most wonderful thing she had ever heard. As the next person started, again she listened so intently.

I have to warn you, when someone really listens to you, you start telling them the truth. That's what happened in that workshop.

When it came near to my turn, I was frantically thinking about my story. I was going to tell something light and unrevealing, with a little humor, and then they would move on to the next person. The problem was, the way she listened, pretty soon all of us were listening intently, and real stories were being told.

When it was my turn, my story felt wrong, and I said, "I have no story." I was very embarrassed, and I waited for them to pass me by. The group just sat quietly and waited. In the tension of the moment, I said, "Can I tell you something that happened recently on our farm?" And they all waited.

I asked, "Have you ever seen forty-five ton of potatoes?" Apparently no one had. I said, "I hadn't either, until this past spring." Then I told them about a community about fifteen miles from our farm, a community named Hollandale. It had, at one time, been a large marsh.

"Some investors bought the land. With dredging machines, they developed a drainage system. Then they divided the area into small farms for growing vegetables. The land was covered with rich peat soil, and was soon settled by people of Dutch descent. It became a rich and prosperous community."

"This year the potato market collapsed. Last year's crop was stored in man-made caves where the temperature was controlled, but the market price was so low the growers couldn't afford to sell their potatoes. The government had a safety net for that kind of situation. It involved buying the crop from the growers at a reduced price. The farmers would make enough so they could continue operating."

"I learned that, because I had a feed lot with three hundred cattle, I qualified for government potatoes to use as feed. All I had to do was sign my name and promise, under penalty, that I would never sell any of those potatoes. One of the categories on that application form was '45 ton', so that was what I circled."

"On a very cold, miserable, rainy March day, the growers started arriving with their dump trucks filled with potatoes. They backed up onto the large slab of dirty cement in our farm yard. The first truck had white potatoes; beautiful, all washed and perfect."

"The grower raised the hoist and all those potatoes rolled out on that dirty cement. There was a government inspector there with his clipboard, taking the weight ticket from the owner so they knew how many pounds of potatoes he was dumping. But, it seemed to make the drivers angry that if there were any red potatoes mixed with the white ones, the reds were discounted. I could see anger in the faces of the men as they drove away. The discounting seemed foolish because the next load would be red potatoes, all washed and perfect, and they would be dumped on the pile with the others. Again, if there were any white potatoes they would be discounted."

"Truck after truck unloaded until I had a pile of fourty-five ton of potatoes. I waited until the growers had all left before I took our big, four-wheel drive loader and started climbing up on the pile to crush them down. They needed to be crushed so that they wouldn't stick in the throats of the cattle and choke them."

As I looked at that circle of people listening, it suddenly occurred to me, and I said, "It seems so amazing to me, because in 1850, my grandfather, as a little boy, got on a sailing ship in Ireland with his family and widowed mother, and headed for America—because they had no potatoes. After a long and frightening journey, they arrived in America. The older boys found work in sweatshops. That widowed mother watched her sons shrinking from the long hours of work, and attending night school. They heard about land further west and they came by wagon train, and settled about five miles from our present farm."

"Years later the youngest boy, my grandfather, moved with his young son and his pregnant wife to the prairie land that he bought from the railroad. With a team of oxen, he broke that sod for the first time. His first crop of wheat arrived in 1876, the year my father was born on the land where we still live. My great-grandmother would have given anything for a bag of potatoes to feed her family. I thought how unusual that her great-grandson, whom she never saw, would someday pile up forty-five ton of potatoes and crush them down to feed to his cattle."

The stories continued around the circle. The leader, Gioia, said, "We have something special going here. I wonder if you would like to eat together." Most everyone agreed and later we gathered at a Pizza Hut. People in the restaurant stared as our group continued telling stories. The workshop had ended at four o'clock that afternoon, and I left the pizza place at eleven that night. We all stood in the parking lot hugging each other, and as I drove my two hours back home, I kept pondering, "What has happened to me?" I felt closer to those people than to neighbors I had known my whole life.

Some of the people in that workshop formed a storytelling group in the Twin Cities area, and sometimes I would join them in putting on a program. If, at the workshop, they had passed me by when I said I had no story, I would never have been able to call myself a storyteller. It was all so random. She had said, "We all need to tell our story," and I found that to be so true. She gave me a new community and changed my life.

The Story of Rose

Rose was a surprise. We'd had three daughters: Michelle, Catherine and Mary. After Mary was born, there were some problems and trips to Mayo Clinic, where we learned that there would be no more children. Farming with a family of three daughters was not the way I had planned life to be, so after some discussion we decided to adopt.

Marty came to us when he was two years old. Two years later, Tom arrived when he was about two months old. Marty and Tom were the same distance apart as my brother and I had been.

I always appreciated having a brother myself, so I was glad the boys had each other. It was a good thing. Tom settled into our routine and everything seemed to be getting comfortable. Our house was just the right size for that many children. Then we found out that we were going to have another baby. We had just decided to add on to our home when my wife's father died unexpectedly in Montana. Then Rose was born a few days before Christmas.

Rose and Tom, just a year apart, became both friends and competitors because they had such different personalities. Tom was short and dark with dark brown eyes, and Rose was tall and slender with blonde hair. She seemed to be born talking, but Tom, on the other hand, was very quiet. Because they were close in age and had so much to do with each other, they seemed to argue and fight about everything.

I used to enjoy going up town with them, because people would stop on the street and ask about those two little children, so different from one another. They were often holding hands, one very dark and square shouldered, the other tall and blonde and skinny. When they would ask, Rose would announce, "This is my brother." Then there would be another puzzled look. How could that be?

I think maybe, because Rose was the youngest, she would often come with me. I enjoyed her company because she said funny things and she could imitate people.

We had a lot of cattle on our farm, and I spent a great deal of time with them. They were rough and wild, and the barn was not a very safe place to be. But up in the hayloft above the barn there were some kittens, and Rose liked to be there. So while I was busy down below treating the cattle, Rose would climb up to the hayloft. I can still see those long skinny legs finding their way up there. With the hubbub of the cattle being moved from pen to pen down below, and the yelling and slamming of gates, I would hear the tempo rise up above, too. Rose would be scolding the kittens as she was trying to get them dressed in doll clothes. She was having about the same amount of trouble as I was, and somehow she always caused me to laugh.

We lived on the home farm, about six miles away from the land we called our North Farm. This was always a very romantic place for me. Where our home farm was flat and conducive to growing crops, the North Farm was hilly and wooded, with original prairie land that had never been broken by the plow. It had a stream running through it, fed by a spring that wound through the hundred acres and emptied into Turtle Creek, a small river on the farm's north border. An annual ritual my entire life included moving a herd of cattle up to the North Farm in the spring, a six mile cattle drive. Then we would bring them home late in the fall, sometimes after a blizzard or the first snow. The North Farm was unusual because of its spring-fed stream, wooded hills and valleys. It offered protection for the cattle, a constant water supply, and plenty of grass for grazing.

When I was a young boy, the farmers who lived around the North Farm were quick to contact us and complain if our cattle got out. That was always an emergency. We had to drop everything, drive up there, try to round them up again, and deal with the angry neighbors. The years passed and times had changed. Most of the land around the North Farm was now owned by absentee landowners. If the cattle got out, we wouldn't hear about it. Sometimes they would just disappear. To solve this problem, I bought a truck that would auger grain into the feed troughs. A couple times a week we would go up and feed the cattle, so if they would break out they didn't run away. They would always hang around, waiting for the feed truck to come in.

Rose was six when this story took place. I think because there were several children in our family, she saw the trip to the North Farm as an opportunity for us to spend an hour or two together. So when she heard that feed truck getting ready to leave, she would come running out and ride along with me.

At that time, an old rickety bridge with plank floors and iron sides crossed Turtle Creek. The weight of the truck was too much for that bridge. We didn't have to cross it; we turned into the pasture right beside it. Then, Rose could walk across the bridge and look at the water, and occasionally there would be people fishing below the bridge.

Sometimes she would come with me and we would look at the cattle, walking among them, making sure they were all right, and counting them.

It was not long 'till Rose met a friend who lived on the other side of the bridge where there were a few houses built into the hills. It was a beautiful area, and this older couple had a retirement home there, along with a big, black dog with a long pointed nose and a bushy tail. He was a collie type dog. His name was Duke, and he and Rose became friends. The truck we were traveling in did not have a good muffler system, and as it was rolling down the hill towards the bridge it made quite a bit of noise.

So this ritual started to happen. Duke would hear the truck coming, and he would bark and start running for the bridge. Rose would say, "Stop, Daddy. Duke is coming!" I would stop and she would jump out of the truck, and start running for the bridge with her long legs. She had hair the color of honey and it would be flowing behind her as she raced towards the bridge. From the other side I would see the dog coming, his black bushy tail floating in the wind. He too was running as fast as he could towards the bridge.

It's a scene I can always see in my mind: this tall, skinny blonde girl and this big, black dog, both racing to meet each other.

They seemed to always meet at the center of the bridge, and they would dance around each other, celebrating their friendship; and then you'd see them running up a hill or pausing to look at something, just enjoying each other and being together. Sometimes the cattle didn't hear the truck; and we had to go and look for them, walking up quite a steep hill. Where the pasture then flattened out, Rose and Duke would be running ahead until they reached a patch of thistles. Thistles are hard on bare feet, and Rose never remembered her shoes. At times I would become impatient and say, "Rose, you are too heavy to carry. Can't you ever remember your shoes?" Duke stood there with his tongue out, watching, and Rose would reply, "Duke will help me."

She'd lie on his back and hang on to his fur coat, and Duke took her right through those thistles. Soon they were together again, running up the hill ahead of me.

When we arrived back at the truck and it was time to go home ('cause Dads are always in a hurry), Rose would pull open the truck door, which seemed to take forever. Duke would jump up on the seat with his tongue out all excited, and Rose would say, "Please, Daddy, he is my very best friend. Can't we take him home?" I'd have to tell her how Duke lived with an older couple, how we had a dog at home who would not like Duke, and how they'd probably fight and it wouldn't work. Then she'd have to get out and hug Duke good-bye, which took forever. It would be the same the next time we went to the North Farm to feed the cattle.

One time, when we were walking up the hill to look for the cattle, I didn't realize they had heard us and they were coming, running through a wooded area. Just as we approached the crest of the hill, a hundred cattle came over the top at a dead run. Duke was terrified. He went like a rocket for home, with Rose running after him screaming,

"Duke, come back. I will save you." She wasn't afraid of those cattle. "Daddy, they are going to kill Duke!" Rose was running and crying, her legs bleeding from the brambles, trying to help her friend. Duke thought speed was the only friend he had, and he was getting out of there.

On another visit to the North Farm, Rose had been to a birthday party at her cousins. She'd saved a piece of birthday cake, and had it wrapped very carefully as she came out to ride with me to the north pasture. She was trying to keep the cake perfect on the trip so she and Duke could share it. When we came to that hill before the bridge, I had to let her out of the truck so she could run very carefully down to meet him. Duke barked, but he didn't come. As I looked up in the distance towards the other hill, I could see that the grandchildren were visiting, and Duke was just too busy playing with them.

Rose ran to the bridge and stood there holding her cake. As I fed the cattle, I could see her crying. When I finished, she climbed slowly into the truck, still holding her piece of cake, and she said, "Duke doesn't love me anymore." And we rode home in silence.

She didn't ride back with me for a few weeks, and then one day she came out and got in the truck. When we got to the hill above the bridge, I saw Duke running. He seemed to be trying to make up for everything. I stopped the truck and said, "Rose, you better go. Duke is coming." She got out of the truck, but she didn't run toward the bridge. She walked, kind of dignified and stiff. Duke got to their meeting place well ahead of her, and he just stood there waiting. Rose walked up, and they acted uncomfortable and formal. They didn't dance around each other and run off to race over the hills; they just stood there awkwardly together.

After I fed the cattle and was ready to go home, Rose walked to the truck and climbed in, and Duke headed for home. It was the first time I had ever seen him walk 'cause he always ran, and that big, black bushy tail was hanging down and seemed to be hitting his heels as he walked. Rose and I headed for home in silence.

I looked over at that little girl sitting beside me. It was an older face now than it had been just a few weeks ago. There was hurt in those eyes. In the silence I realized I had just seen a love die, and it was no one's fault.

Cape May

It was almost magic. The call came from a stranger. He had talked to my daughter and said he was from New Jersey, a place called Cape May. She had gotten the message some confused, and that's the reason I called him back.

He said his name was Tim Albrecht, but it was his voice that I noticed. It was so gentle. As we talked, and the conversation started innocently enough, he said that a district judge from their court system had traveled to the National Storytelling Festival at Jonesborough, Tennessee. He had seen me perform there and had brought my tapes back to New Jersey. These tapes were now being used in therapy sessions to help terminally ill people feel safe enough to share their stories. My stories seemed to prompt these people, many of whom were very young, to begin telling their experiences of living with the AIDS virus, or with cancer.

It was a magical phone call. Tim said that he was a social worker in Cape May County. He spoke with such compassion as he talked about these special people, and I imagined that's how Mother Theresa would sound on the phone.

He said, "We are like a leper colony here. No one wants to look at us. Oftentimes, because the treatment is so expensive, families have to abandon their relatives so that the state and county will take over. Many times gay couples are the only ones with the kind of commitment that will keep these AIDS victims in their homes."

He said that he wanted to thank me for my stories, and he just wanted me to know that, somehow, they were making a difference. Our conversation would have ended, except I asked him, almost without intending to, if he would like me to come there. His response was, "Would you?" Because his question was a surprise to me, I said, without really thinking, "Yes."

When we say, "Yes," sometimes we change our lives. I think that's what happened this time.

Months later, and after many phone calls back and forth, I flew to Cape May. It was June 17, 1993. I was flying there with mixed emotions, feeling that somehow I was going to change something. Maybe I would make up for the fact that my nephew, Richie, had died of AIDS almost a year earlier.

It had been the wettest, coldest spring in the last hundred years and our farm was still half unplanted; so I, too, felt very vulnerable.

In the many conversations with Tim, we had planned a workshop format to be held in a safe, comfortable setting. Then we decided to ask Fred Silverman, a film director from New York, to tape the stories shared that day. I had worked with Fred in 1989 at the National Storytelling Festival in Jonesborough,

Tennessee.

Tim was, at first, reluctant to have the AIDS victims filmed. He called them "these fragile people." But I was able to convince him that Fred was a very sensitive man and that he would be the right one to make this movie.

I had a lot of weight on my shoulders as I left home. One time, Tim had called me and said in an emphatic voice, "I think I'm going crazy. I'm talking to a farmer in Minnesota, whom I don't know. Now he's introduced me by phone to a film maker in New York, and they are both coming to my town to put on a program among some very fragile people who I do know. And when I talk to my co-workers, they say, 'What a marvelous idea' and I am so afraid. This is a leap of faith." And that's exactly how that went.

Tim met me at the plane in Atlantic City, and I remember the way we looked at each other. His eyes were round, but they were gentle and very probing. As we drove along, two strangers who recognized each other only by their voices, I studied him and he would turn and look at me like we had a lot of catching up to do.

He asked me if I would like to stop at the strip to do a little gambling. I was surprised and laughed, and he laughed at the same time. We agreed that we thought we were doing enough gambling by what we were planning to do.

On the way to his home, we stopped by the Atlantic Ocean and walked barefooted on the beach. I'd only seen the Atlantic once in my life and that was under very different circumstances. As we walked in silence, and I watched this thick-set serious man in that powerful setting, there was a sense of awe that swept over me. We just stood and looked across that body of water. Almost no words were spoken.

Then we looked at each other and walked towards the car, dusted the sand off of our feet, put on our shoes, and drove to his home.

On Friday morning I met the other part of the team: Julie, a harpist from Philadelphia, and Vicki, a group coordinator and therapist from Eslan, California. I also learned, because of the intensity of the workshop and the fragile condition of the people participating, there would be medical doctors, counselors and therapists in attendance at all times.

The morning was very intense, with Vicki and Julie and I getting to know each other. Now, as I look back on it, Tim stayed in the background. Very nervous, he served us tea, and stayed out of the conversation. I realized, that morning, that the four of us each had a dream of what we hoped to do, and now it was time to make those dreams mesh together.

I was excited by the power in that room.

Friday afternoon was spent in a park, filming with the camera crew and Fred Silverman, a creative artist, an intense, sensitive, yet probing interviewer. He asked me questions between the jet plane flights overhead, when we would have to shut down. He asked me to reach inside myself to find answers to questions, like, "What does a farmer from Minnesota hope to do with these people?" and "Why are you a storyteller?"

After trying to answer those questions on camera, I began to realize the true scope of this mission. Later, Fred drove me to the Wetlands Institute, the place where the workshop would be held. It is a federal building in a great marshy area, a filtering bed between the ocean and the mainland, where serious looking conservationists explore and document balances of nature. Three sides of this institute overlook the water. In the conference room of the Wetlands Institute, the tall windows that gave the view of the marsh were being covered, and cameras and lights were being set up. Power cables and duct tape seemed to be everywhere. The camera crew was getting ready for the filming that evening.

My stomach was just beginning to relax from the filming in the park, but it went back into high gear. I realized that all of this lighting and all of those cameras were to film something so important, and I didn't know how it was going to work.

The lighting and sound technicians, and others on the filming crew, were asking me where this light should be, and where I was going to stand, and what I was going to do. I didn't know the answers to these questions.

According to the plan, Friday evening was going to be a one hour presentation of stories on camera. The audience would be local people, professional staff, and friends who were interested in, and supportive of this program.

I watched the people coming in, all strangers to me. Yet, as they greeted me, I knew that many of them recognized my voice from those taped stories. They came in walking dutifully, like they were supporting a good cause. Then, as they stepped across those power cables and saw the cameras and lights on the stage, their heads came up, and their shoulders came back, and they got a sparkle about them that said, "This must be quite an event. Aren't we lucky we came!" They brought a real spirit as they took their places.

Standing in the background and being introduced to person after person, I was concerned that much of the success of this program, or the failure, depended on me. The room filled up, and there was excitement in the air.

A wonderful surprise was the addition to the program of a singing group, three young men from Johannesburg, South Africa. They sang with style and with passion songs about peace and justice, and things that people have always longed for. They brought South Africa to that room that night, and they did it with passion and with charm.

I shared farm stories that were light and humorous and vulnerable, connecting kinds of stories that bridged the distance between us. My stories told these people who I am, but more importantly, I wanted them to know how valuable their own stories are.

The evening passed quickly. The audience was responsive and everything went well. It was late when we left, but the team stopped to visit the ocean. Alone on the beach, just the five of us, I had that sense of power and the deep commitment that I had felt the day before.

It was now almost midnight, and it was agreed that whoever wanted to would meet there again at daylight. We would join together in meditation and prayer before we started the workshop. Even though I was very tired, I knew I would be there, and the others said they would, too.

The next morning, just as the sun was peeking over the horizon, fourteen people gathered, surrounded by fog and the roar of the ocean. We formed a circle and we all joined arms. Whoever wanted to spoke, and we each told why we had come. In the silence, and in the ocean sound, we realized we had come from all parts of the country, and we had come to be a part of something special.

Then we took ten minutes to walk in solitude on that empty beach, each alone with his or her thoughts. Someone pointed out to me the dolphins playing far in the distance. They said this was a good omen. The dolphins are hardly ever seen this close to shore.

After our walk we came back in silence, stood in a circle, and asked for strength and the power of each other to join together in our quest. This was a very special time for me. Then we drove back to the Wetlands Institute. There was a bustle of activity again as the cameras were readied. Some of the workshop participants were beginning to arrive, as well as the professional support team of doctors, counselors, and therapists. In my mind I can still see the Spanish doctor, as she wept with frustration at a system where people could not afford to be sick.

The purpose of this whole thing was simple. We were to create a safe place where these people, who were terminally ill and very vulnerable, would feel free to tell their stories.

Julie's gentle, inviting harp music was a perfect way to open the session. During my story, I watched as those people connected themselves to the vulnerability and strength of the tiny bird who had confronted the huge tractor. Then we each introduced ourselves and told a little story of how we'd gotten our names. It was time for applause, because everyone there had just told a personal story. Then we took a little break, the first of several planned for the comfort of the group.

In that break time, one young man got word to me that he might, he just might, tell a story, but no one else volunteered.

The morning went on and Julie's music became a part of my stories. Earlier, she had put out a variety of percussion instruments, and she told us that she needed us to empower her music with the beat. After each break, Julie would encourage the workshop participants to pick up any instrument of their choice.

I noticed that each time they took up the beat, it got much stronger. I noticed, too, how Julie, with her eyes and her endless smile, with the way her fingers danced across the harp, with every fiber in her body, was pulling the people toward her. The energy she had out there was incredible.

Throughout the morning, Vicki moved around the backside of the room, like she was taking the pulse of the group. At times she would call my attention to one person. She seemed to be quietly keeping the group centered, like she was almost breathing life into it, although very much behind the scenes.

After the noon break, it was time for everyone to begin sharing their own stories. I said I would lead off, and then anyone who wanted to could follow. By this time there was a sense of community in the air. Everyone was smiling, and as they picked up the beat there were no more timid participants. The beat became a sound that you could feel in your body.

The youngest person at the workshop was named Nat. He was eleven years old, going on forty. He needed someone with him all of the time. Three years earlier, he was diagnosed with cancer of the cerebellum, and since that time he had endured many surgeries. His face showed the effects of that experience.

His friend and helpmate was a young man who had been a Marine Lieutenant in Viet Nam. His hair was prematurely white. He just seemed to have such tenderness toward Nat. Nat had very thick glasses. Talking with him was like talking with a forty year old, only he was more honest.

Nat said, "I don't have a lot of strength. I may not be able to stay to the end of this, so I need to tell my story now." He told of how he wished kids would treat him as if he was ordinary, instead of unusual, how he wished younger children would look up to him and older children would treat him kindly. Instead, he said, kids his age made fun of him and treated him like a freak. He just wished that all of them would treat him like he was ordinary. In our group he had many friends—probably his best friend was Mike the Marine from Viet Nam.

Mike smiled and beamed like it was the best compliment he had ever received. Nat opened the gate. One by one, people came forward. The stories were real and they were powerful. They were told with tears both from the tellers and the listeners.

Nobody saw the big cameras as they turned in on the tellers.

At one point, I noticed one of the cameramen with a long camera on his shoulder. As he swung around to zero in on the speaker, I saw a tear running down the cameraman's cheek.

The participants told things like how they could thank God for this disease, that it was the only way they could have learned how to live. I think we all began to realize that the sick weren't the ones that needed this workshop. This was for the world, and we were only the vehicle to get it there.

Twenty-one of the twenty-two participants shared their stories that day. The doctors and the therapists did not want to be left out, so they, too, told their stories. In the Wetlands Institute on that Saturday afternoon, we were not workshop people, participants, and helpers. We were human beings, meeting and communicating on a deep level.

As the workshop drew to a close, I asked a woman with curly hair and a husky voice if she wanted to add anything. She was the only one who had not told her story. She looked to be in perfect health and she had such a spirit about her. She shook her head and said she had nothing to add.

It was time to start our good-byes. I looked at these people, with whom I had become so closely attached, and I said, "This has been such an incredible experience for me." Then I brought a plastic bag from my briefcase and said, "These are soybeans from my farm and from my combine. Soybeans are healthy if you want to eat them, and they will grow if you want to plant them. The market is quite low now, so feel free to take as many as you want. We, most likely, will never meet again. I want to leave you with a seed to remind you that you have an important story to tell. I want to thank all of you for the experience we have had." The bag was passed around and everyone took their seeds.

By four p.m. the workshop was over, but no one was leaving. To take a break from the intensity, I walked out by the water to try to think about what had just happened there. Almost immediately, the woman who hadn't shared her story was standing beside me.

She said, "You wanted me to tell my story. I know you did. But I couldn't do it there. I'm going to tell you now."

For the next half hour she told me the story of her life. Her name was Ann. She was thirty-five years old. She was the mother of two daughters. She didn't think she would live long enough to see them marry. She was dying of AIDS. She told me of her dreams, and her fears, of how she was going to leave her children. She said that she would not give up "the truth" in the time that she had left, and here's the example she gave.

She said, "I want to take care of my teeth, so having moved to a new area I was looking for a dentist. I filled out the information form and when I came to the question regarding the HIV virus, I marked 'yes.' In a few moments a man in a white coat came out and said, 'I'm sorry. We are not able to help you; our insurance … You will have to go somewhere else.' I left the office, and at the next dentist's office the same thing happened. I was determined not to stray from the truth, and finally I found one who said, 'Come in. We can help you.'"

As she spoke, I noticed how her green eyes seemed to change color, just like the breaking waves of the Atlantic Ocean, and I saw her as a very heroic person. When she finished, we were both in tears.

Fred Silverman had hoped to get personal interviews with many of the workshop participants. Our concern was that the day had been so exhausting, and they would not have enough strength to go on camera again. The staff was amazed that no one refused his request. In fact, they seemed to welcome it.

The workshop was over. And gradually, gradually the people left. Even Nat had not left early. Later, some of us walked back to the ocean. Again in silence, we stood in a circle to thank whatever power it was had brought us together.

No one was willing to let the day end, so we gathered at Tim's house for dinner in the garden. It was the most unusual night of my life. People kept coming to me with their stories, even people who had not been part of this thing at all. Many of the stories were very tragic—of families torn apart by the HIV virus, and the rage toward the relatives who brought it in, of pain at family gatherings.

Some wanted to ask how you told stories, and some just wanted to talk about things that were very important to them. Tim asked me if I would tell a story to the group, because some of the guests had not been to the Friday night program or the workshop. When I stood up to tell that last story, I realized that I was so exhausted that I didn't even know how it went. I muddled through it, but no one seemed to mind. It must have been almost two in the morning when I finally went to bed. I knew that I had to be up early the next morning for one last interview on camera, and then I would fly out later in the afternoon.

Fred Silverman picked me up at nine a.m. I had a doughnut and a cup of coffee in the car. Fred's wife, Sharon, and a member of the camera crew brushed my hair and fixed me up.

The sun was coming up hot over the Wetlands. The camera crew, in between the roar of the boats, tried to capture the sounds of some low flying deep water birds as I answered questions like, "Are you satisfied with what happened yesterday?" "What was your goal for this project?" "Why are you here?"

After the filming, I went back to the house and woke Tim so he could take me to the airport in Atlantic City. We drove along in almost total silence, both into our own thoughts. Looking over at him and thinking about his gentle intensity, I said, "Tim, where in the hell did you come from?" He looked at me with those eyes that are so round and so probing, and he said, "Are you sure you want to know?" I was a little taken aback and I was not sure, but I answered, "Yes, I do want to know."

He said, "I started out as a drug dealer. I was not going to work the way my father had in the steel mills all his life. I was going to be smart and take the easy way, so in college I began to deal drugs. Then, to keep out of Viet Nam, I chose working in a military psyche unit in Texas where I dealt with the wounded coming back from Nam. Their arms and legs were gone and they were nuts. When I left there I was so angry and distraught,

I knew I had to do something for these people who were unable to help themselves. And that is my story."

At the airport, Tim and I hugged each other. I said that we may never meet again, but neither one of us believed that. We had done something very powerful together. I got on the plane. As it was taking off, I thought of him and all the people I'd met and all the stories I'd heard. I began to cry. I cried the whole flight and couldn't seem to stop.

I returned to the wet fields of Minnesota and we finished our planting by early July. As a crop year, 1993 was looked upon as a disaster for farmers in the Midwest. But for me, 1993 brought my chance to understand, and to really feel the healing power of stories.

I went to help the people in Cape May, New Jersey. They changed my life forever.

Great Ideas

Oftentimes my stories are about horses. And when I tell to older groups, people will come up with their own memories, their own stories. This happened recently when a man came up and told me about his brother.

He said, "My younger brother always had such big ideas. He would get these good ideas; and you know, he never amounted to nothin'." Then he started his story.

He told me that when he was about thirteen and his brother was two years younger, a big cow had died on their farm. The custom, then, was to skin the hide off the cow before it was buried. About every farm kid knew how to do it, and about every farm kid hated that job.

Their dad said that he had some business to do up town, and he wanted the boys to skin the cow while he was gone. It was a hot morning. The cow was lying out in the pasture where they were to work on it. They started by skinning the back legs and the back, and then moving forward, keeping the hide all in one piece and not having any noticeable cut marks. It was a slow, smelly and disagreeable job. They'd been at it about an hour when his brother had one of his great ideas. He suggested that they skin along the stomach so the hide was open to the front legs, and he bet that if they got that good team of horses their dad had, and tied a rope to that hide, that team of horses would pull the hide off of that cow.

"It sounded like too good an idea. It was a hot day, and I thought about it for a while. I thought, if it would even take half the hide off, it would save us a lot of time." That team of horses was their dad's pride and joy. They were not only well matched, they were smart and well behaved. He could always trust them and count on them to do the right thing. The boys brought the team down to the pasture with a rope to tie the horses to the partially skinned cow. When they got the horses near the cow, the smell of the cow and the blood made the horses spooky, and they got nervous. But the brothers backed them up, and hooked the rope to the hide and to the double-tree evener behind the horses.

When the horses started to pull, it worked even better than the brothers had thought. There was a loud ripping sound, and that hide ripped right off the cow 'til it got to the front end, where they had stopped skinning. But . . . the loud ripping sound was a noise that the horses had never heard before, and they took off running. The older brother held on to the lines as long as he could, trying to run, eventually being dragged, and he finally had to let go. He said, "I'll never forget the sight of those horses racing across the pasture with that cow and the front part of the hide still hooked to it, and the carcass bouncing across the field as they galloped, trying to run away from that cow."

They went through a fence, and that's where the cow and hide stopped. The horses raced down the road for the barn, and both ran in the door that the boys had forgotten to shut when they'd gotten them out.

Then he said, "When my dad came home, we were frantically trying to get the door frame loose where his prize team was jammed together. One of the horses was crippled. I don't think Dad ever forgave my brother."

By this time, the man was standing in front of me with a very sad look on his face as the memories came back. He said, "You know, my brother would always have these ideas. I just can't understand it. He never amounted to nothin."

Pardon Me, Mouse

In the fifty plus years I've driven a combine, often at
night a little field mouse runs ahead of me between the soybean
rows. He is confused by the lights focused on him and he doesn't
seem to know where to run or where he is safe. It's a very small
incident in the operation of the harvest, but I wanted to write a
poem, looking at it from both his side and my side.

> First I see your shadow.
> You begin your frantic flight,
> Rushing headlong down the row,
> In the glare of combine lights.
>
> You look so frail and tiny,
> Beneath the frosty plants.
> I hope you had time to dress,
> Put on some warmer pants.
>
> I wonder for your family,
> Were they hidden all back there?
> Why are you so alone?
> What story could you share?

I wonder how you feel,
Whatever can you trust?
Pursued by a lighted monster,
That grinds your world to dust.

When you start to tire,
Your pelt of white and tan
Draws near the flashing sickle.
You have no escape plan.

I slow the racing combine,
Before it pulls you in.
You slip into the darkness,
Maybe to flee again.

I wonder, was it your kin,
Running in that same bean row,
While driving my first combine,
Over fifty years ago?

The stories passed down to you,
Probably made you feel safe.
Tales of slow old combines,
Mice that ran and won the race.

Each year I wonder
If yours and mine will meet?
Or has there been just too much change?
You're not able to compete.

Maybe, it will be different,
At some future date.
Yours will be attending.
Mine, the empty place.

I wish for a social meeting,
Not this yearly race.
Maybe sipping tea together,
Or sharing in the grace.

We could talk about this field,
What it means to you and me.
Make plans for the future.
Talk of harmony.

We have these annual meetings.
You scurry through frosty air.
I watch from a modern combine.
You, small and fragile there.

This yearly scene,
Draws from me a sigh.
Can you, a fragile mouse,
Outlast this combine and I?

Graduation Story

The story begins with a phone call from a school superintendent in the small town of Lyle, Minnesota, right on the Iowa border. The superintendent asked me if I would be the graduation speaker for the class of that year, 1999. This came as quite a shock and surprise to me because—I don't know how it is where you live, but where I live—farmers are not asked to be graduation speakers.

As the conversation went on, he said, "Usually, we get someone who talks way over their heads; the kids are into their own thing and how they look, and they are excited, and they don't remember one thing that the speaker says. Because you are a storyteller," he continued, "I believe you can engage them and give them something memorable."

I was very flattered and very nervous. I know you can't preach to kids on their graduation night, and I tried to think of what story I had that might work. No matter how often I thought about it, nothing came to mind. All I could think of was an incident that had happened on our farm just a few weeks earlier. So that night, I told this story for the first time.

It's a great honor for me to be here tonight to talk to the Class of 1999, the class that will lead us into a new century. Eighteen thousand, two hundred and fifty dollars; does that sound like a lot to you? When I was your age, it would build a pretty nice house. Now, eighteen thousand, two hundred and fifty dollars would buy a pretty good used car. Eighteen thousand two hundred and fifty is the number of days between our ages.

If you remember, we have had a very wet spring on the farm. There was a lot of frustration trying to get the crop planted, and on one of these days I said to my son, Tom, "We have a wet spot right south of the farmstead where there is water standing. Why don't we take the tile plow, and you and Leroy chain those two big tractors together and pull the tile line into that spot."

He said, "We won't be able to raise anything on it then."

I said, "Nothing will grow on it anyway. At least we will have it drained for next year."

Because it was a beautiful day, I wanted to drive around the borders of the farm. I planned to take a smaller tractor and drive out across the fields. Before I left, Tom asked me, "Where does the underground power come into the farm?" I showed him where I thought it was. I also needed to leave because I could see those two big, four wheel drive tractors, with mud flying out from between their dual wheels, spinning and roaring as they tried to pull the tile plow through the wet area in the field. It was not a pleasant sight and I wanted to get away from it.

Before I got out of the farmyard with my tractor, Tom's wife, Alma, came running from the house. Her black hair was sudsy with shampoo and her black eyes flashed in anger.

She said, "Where's Tom?"

I said, "Well, he's out in the field, but what's the problem?"

She answered, "The water went off, and I'm supposed to be at a meeting." I gave her a number to call to check if the electricity was off locally or if it was a widespread outage. Then I drove away, happy that I didn't have to face those angry eyes.

When I got out in the far corner of the field, estimating when we could start working the soil for planting, I saw a truck coming down the road with a flashing light on it. I thought, "That must be the electrical company." I continued on my way, and then I saw another truck coming. All of a sudden, I realized that I had told Tom where the power entered the farm underground twenty-five years ago, instead of where it had been rerouted for the new transformer just a couple of years earlier.

My quiet time was over. I opened the throttle and headed for home. There were major problems.

If life ever seems dull and boring, and you need some excitement, you can really change it by just cutting an underground power line.

When I came into the farmyard, it was filled with trucks. They all had lights flashing, and the crackle of two-way radios was echoing around the yard. There was chaos everywhere. This white haired man was screaming at Tom, and Tom, who is normally quiet, was yelling, "You have to calm down so I can calm down." And then he saw me and said, "There's my Dad. You can talk to him, now."

The white haired man looked at me and hollered something about how we were going to have to pay for everything and that there were many people without power now. Then he brought me over to his truck, where the two-way radio was blaring, so I could talk to his boss. Before I got on the radio, I said to him, "There's one thing about it. It's my fault. I'm the one who made the mistake."

I didn't realize until afterwards that something changed, but then I heard his boss say, "This is all going on your bill. The line is cut in several places, and we are going to call in equipment to repair it." I was surprised when the white haired man interceded for me and said, "He is the owner, and he knows it," 'cause his boss was still yelling.

By now, the workers were checking the ground with a tester, looking for where the line was cut. They discovered that it had only been cut in one place instead of many, but the man on the radio kept saying, "We need this backhoe, and this digging machine that is twenty miles away and I am going to call for it to come in."

I said, "You don't need to bring it. We have a backhoe right here. We have all the equipment that you need, and I have nothing better to do than to run it for you." Then I asked him if he could please get some of these trucks out of here because they were all just standing around.

Tom told me that he had called all of the neighbors that were affected, and told them that we would have the power back on before too long. Meanwhile, Tom's little boy, who was about two and a half, came out. As we were bringing the backhoe around to start digging, he wanted to get up on the tractor with me. Where I was having a terrible day, Brandon was having a wonderful day. With all the trucks, all the noise and two-way radios, his eyes were like saucers watching it all. Normally Brandon wanted to be with his Dad all of the time, but when Tom wanted to take him up town, because they weren't able to fix dinner, Brandon wasn't leaving for anything.

Tom and Alma had been trying to show me that Brandon could talk in sentences, but every time they would ask him, he wouldn't do it. He would just say a word or two. When I asked one of the men to move his truck so I could get the tractor in there, Brandon said, "No, Bompa! That him's truck!" And he pointed a little two year old finger at another man. Brandon knew what was going on.

The trucks began leaving the yard. With Brandon sitting between my knees, we started digging in the ground for the broken power line. The white haired man that had been in charge, told me that he had not had any breakfast. He'd had a terrible morning, and he wondered if I would mind if he went and ate his lunch. I said, "That will be fine. Brandon and I will dig it out."

A calm settled over the farm. As we dug the trench with water in it, we located the cable and had it ready. Another man drove in. He was the one that was there to splice the line.

As he got down in that water and began his work, he looked like a surgeon doing an operation.

After coming back from his lunch, the white haired man said to me, now very calm, "That sure is a cute little boy."

Maybe because of all that had happened, I said to him, "He is a very important little boy. You see, his Dad is adopted, and this little boy is the only blood relative that he has. I am so afraid that if anything would happen to Brandon, I don't know that my son, Tom, could handle it."

Then he walked back to his truck. The man in the trench finished joining the line and put a rubber boot over the connection. Then he heated that rubber with a torch and it looked just like the line had never been broken.

He finished his work, and he supervised while Brandon and I replaced the dirt in the trench. I thanked him, and he drove away.

The white haired foreman came back from his pickup, and he asked if my son was coming back. I said, "I don't know. He will be back, but it might be an hour or two."

He said, "I wish I could talk to him. I was called out at six this morning and I have had nothing but problems, and I took it out on him." He said, "Your son handled the situation more maturely than I did, and I would like to tell him I am sorry." Then he told me how he was going to retire shortly, and how his daughter was adopting a child from Russia, how she had to wait until it was six weeks old before she could bring it here, how he and his wife were going to fly to Russia with her to meet their first grandchild, and how excited they were.

I knew that when you adopt, there is always a story. I told him that I was glad that he thought Tom handled the situation well, because I am depending on him to run this farm someday. He said, "I think he will be very capable. Would you just tell him that I am very sorry for the way I acted?"

I said, "I will, and I am sure he will understand."

He said, "That sure is a cute little boy," and then he drove away.

I want to share with you something as you graduate, so you will know it now; because I just learned it recently.

You are the class of 1999, and you will be the leaders of the next century. I believe you have a date with destiny, and I believe you are equal to it because you are such good listeners.

Eighteen thousand two hundred and fifty; that's how many days there are between your graduation and mine. I will be having my fiftieth class reunion this summer. Eighteen thousand two hundred and fifty days between us, and what I recently learned is: so much of what happens in each of those days depends on what *you yourself* bring to it.

It has been an honor for me to be your speaker.

People of the Earth

One winter night several years ago, I was attending an event on the third floor of St. Stephen's Church School in the inner city of Minneapolis, Minnesota. As I passed by the first floor, I noticed a large group of people forming lines, plates in hand, and waiting for food to be served. The desolate of the city were being fed.

It was a bitter, cold night in January, and there was an excitement in the room that happens when warm food and hungry people come together.

As I left the school later that evening, the dinner was finished and the people in charge were trying to put everything away. But many of the partakers remained sitting in the hallways, and huddled in the corners, quietly resisting going out into the night. I wondered if they had a place to go.

A high percentage of those remaining were Native Americans. I couldn't help but notice how out of place they looked, and that their faces were almost without expression.

During the two hour drive home on that cold night, I kept reflecting back on the scene at that church hall. I realized these people were people of the earth, whose ancestors had lived for many thousands of years in harmony with that earth. These were people who seemed to know, in their very being, that you only take what you need, always leaving enough for the needs of tomorrow's children. I believe that these are secrets of survival that we so desperately need to relearn.

We, the farmers, followed them, and we have inherited the job as caretakers of the land. Even though we live in different generations, and experience different situations, we—like the Native Americans who came before—have to live in harmony with the seasons and with the plants and animals these seasons produce.

The memory of that cold, January evening haunts me yet. In my mind I see the expressionless faces of those people standing in that inner city food line. These once proud people seemed misplaced. The wisdom of their ancestors, who called plants and animals brothers, is useless here.

The image I'd had of the Native Americans was so different. I remember stories of the Indians of the forest, how they could move through without rustling a leaf or breaking a twig. It was like they became a part of the very forest itself.

I pictured the Plains Indian: that lean, muscular young man riding on a buffalo hunt or riding into battle on a pony. In the scenes of battle, that Indian hung down along the flank of his pony; his foot held by one leather thong, his body totally shielded by the horse, in a full-speed gallop shooting his weapon from beneath the pony's neck. I've ridden horses bareback. I know the discipline, training and the physical strength it would take to perform such a feat.

It was difficult to match these images I had with the people huddled in the corners at that school in Minneapolis. These were people whose ancestors gave their children names like Running Deer or Prairie Flower, names expressing hope that their children would learn to live in harmony with nature. After all, these were people who knew their very lives came from the earth.

On our farm, I believe the corn plant is probably the most human of all the crops I grow. Year after year we see the corn plant start as a very tender shoot, seeming almost too fragile for its environment. In a relatively short time, that stalk stands eight to ten feet tall and looks like it will live forever.

Yet we know, when the chill air of autumn comes, that strong plant will shrivel and die. When we harvest it, the stalk itself will seem small and insignificant, holding out only its grain—that ear of corn—for us to harvest.

Each year we, the people of the earth, watch this corn plant go through its stages, starting as a fragile seedling and growing quite slowly until it reaches knee high. Then it becomes so powerful. The leaves grow broad, and the plant seems to shoot heavenward until it reaches its most dramatic stage.

At that point it puts out a tassel, sets an ear, and the air becomes heavy with the smell of pollen as the corn is in full-scale reproduction. Though we watch all these stages with joy and hope, when the winter winds blow and the harvest is complete, no one is going to say, "Wasn't that corn magnificent when it was knee high?" or "Wasn't that corn great when it was tasseling and putting on the ear?" When the winter winds blow and the earth sleeps, all they will say about that corn crop is, "What did it yield?"

People of the earth, whether they be farmers, Native Americans, or others who work closely with the land experiencing this annual life cycle, are unable to merge this wisdom with today's bottom line value system, where accumulation and consumption are the goals. The earth's well-being is not included in this equation. People who hold this earth-wisdom often fall victim to this conflict of values.

As long as corn has been grown, the people who grow it know deep within their being that when the epitaph is written, they, like the corn crop, will be remembered with the same words, "What did they yield?"

Dodging Retirement

It is quite a challenge to be getting older and holding my position as a co-boss and co-manager on a modern working farm. This was made clear to me when I was seventy-seven years old, during the hustle of fall harvesting.

I first ran a combine in 1949 when I was eighteen. Over the years, I bought a whole series of combines from the 1950s into the 1990s, when I turned over responsibility for purchasing farm machinery. The last combine I bought was in the mid-1980s during what was known as the Farm Crisis. It was a big machine and worked really well. I ran it for many years. I knew it so well that I responded automatically to its quirks. We were like old friends who knew what to expect from each other.

My son, Tom, who is managing the farm now, bought the combine that we are using now in 2008. It is quite different from the one I was used to, but I really wanted to keep my job as a "fill-in" operator.

It was a beautiful fall day and the soybean harvest was in full swing. Tom wanted to leave for a couple of hours, so he gave me a quick set of instructions for running the new combine.

I nodded to let him know that I understood, and that he was leaving the machine with an "experienced" operator.

This combine took ten rows of soybeans at a time, whereas the previous one had taken six. It moved at four miles an hour where the other one had moved at two. There were many automatic controls that needed monitoring, and I was trying to watch them and get used to the faster speed as I scanned the twenty-five foot head and watched for any obstructions or rocks that might be hidden in the rows. The field is a half mile long, and when I made the mile-long round trip and came back to where the truck sat, it was time to dump the three hundred bushel holding tank.

The first thing needing to be done was to push a switch that moved the twenty foot long unloading auger from its normal position, parallel with the combine. Then, that big auger would swing out at a ninety degree angle over the truck. The next step was to engage that auger with a lever that worked just the opposite from the old combine that I had run.

This auger would unload the three hundred bushel holding tank in about three minutes. Then the operator would shut it off. With the push of a button, that big auger would swing back to position parallel with the combine. Then it was time to drive back to the bean rows; again push a couple more switches, and the combine would start the threshing machine again.

Above the operator was a monitor with a series of lights

that came on, and as he approached the bean rows, before he reached the traveling speed, all the lights would disappear as each part of the machine got up to its operating speed.

Meanwhile, the operator would be busy watching the front-end of the combine getting positioned on those ten rows, watching that big header operating its automatic height control, seeing that the beans were flowing into the combine and that there were no rocks or obstructions in its path.

On my combines, for almost sixty years, there had been no automatic equipment; everything moved at a much slower pace. That October day in 2008, I had run the new machine for maybe an hour or so, and was just starting to feel comfortable with it. It seemed like I was going to be able to handle it. About half way through my shift on the combine, I was starting to perfect the unloading time, and I had everything in position as I was backing toward the truck. I was actually thinking I was doing a pretty good job at mastering this complicated machine.

I finished unloading the holding tank and was starting back down the field, bringing everything up to speed and watching carefully that all those ten rows of beans were feeding into the combine. I looked up at the monitor overhead and was shocked to see one of the warning lights still flashing. I wasn't able to read what it said between flashes, so I had to wipe the dust off of my bifocals as I was driving, only to see that the message on the monitor was "Unloading Auger." Panic!

I had folded the auger back to its transport position parallel to the machine, but I had not shut it off. This auger, that could unload three hundred bushel in three minutes, was busy unloading beans and spilling them back on the bare ground.

I knew there would be a stream of bright, cream colored soybeans beans lying in that black dirt in a row behind the combine. Because the cab was so soundproof, and the unload control was just opposite of the one I used to run, I had not heard the auger running. Since the soybeans were laying in a row in the field I had just harvested, they would be almost impossible to pick up. My first thought, like any career politician who wants to keep his job after making a mistake, was, "Cover it up, so no one will notice." I figured, if I backed up and started over again, and only took five rows instead of ten rows, that the bean straw and chaff would fall directly on my stream of beans laying in the field and no one would notice.

It took a bit of time to get my rows right and maneuver that combine around to cover up my mistake. I would have to go that full mile round trip, before the rows would be even and unnoticeable. Much to my relief, I had the field straightened out and everything working well by the time my son returned. I felt pretty good now, because he would not notice my mistake.

He immediately asked, "Is that all you got done?" He then asked me how I got along with the machine, and I gave him pretty short answers. He asked, "How did it work for you?" and I said, "Not too bad," kinda letting him know there really was no problem getting familiar with this machine. "Not too bad," sounds a lot more honest than, "Wonderful!"

As he climbed up into the combine and I got in the pickup, again I had a good feeling. No one would know. As I was driving away I looked back, and instead of the machine moving swiftly down the field with everything working perfectly, Tom was running toward me, waving his arms and yelling. What could be wrong to cause that kind of excitement?

What I had forgotten was that this new combine was equipped with Global Positioning Monitoring. What he had in his hand, as he was running and yelling, was a detailed map of all my maneuverings. The map disclosed everything. Like a real tattletale, it disclosed my creative maneuvering. Two extra half mile trips back and forth across the field, and a loss of time and energy and profit. It reminded me of President Nixon's Watergate tapes. I was caught, due to technology, and I would be relegated to the position of "questionable" combine operator.

I only took one lesson from this experience. The lesson wasn't that I should be more honest about mistakes that made me feel old. The lesson I learned was that next time, when you are going to be creative, be sure and shut off that GPS so there will be no damning evidence!

Reading Group Extras

Biography

Michael Cotter was born near Austin, Minnesota, in 1931 on the farm that had been in his family since 1876. He was the youngest of eight children and was raised in a strict Irish-Catholic household. However, the barn and fields were a different world, populated by hired men who were hoboes, drifting in during the Great Depression. His stories reflect those two conflicting life styles, blended together with his own version of Irish humor.

Michael has farmed with horses and combines with global positioning; and his stories describe the personalities of the people and animals that were a part of that evolution.

He was fifty years old when he first stepped on the stage, and his unusual approach to storytelling has given him the opportunity to perform throughout the U.S.; including the Smithsonian Folk Festival, National Storytelling Festival, schools, fairs, retreats, programs, television, hosting radio shows in Des Moines, Iowa, and Austin, and a number of other venues. He was the Artistic Director of the Minnesota

Storytelling Festival for twenty-two years, starred in a healing stories film used by the Mayo Clinic, and is a national award winning storyteller.

Michael now resides in Albert Lea, Minnesota, with his wife Beverly, a writer and artist, and still spends his days working with his son on the farm.

Questions and Answers
with Author Michael Cotter

Why do you tell stories?

Because I need to. I want to preserve a time in history that I lived in, and the people and feelings that were a part of that time. An example of that is a hobo named Hank, a WWI veteran and alcoholic, who worked on our farm when I was a little boy. I remember a Tuesday morning, when a saloon keeper brought Hank back out to the farm. He had been gone for three days. He was hung over and vulnerable, and he had drunk up next month's wages. The saloon keeper came to collect, and my dad was furious; and he was not going to pay. Two very angry, strong willed men came together; each one just knowing he was right. My mother slipped a check to the tavern owner, and diffused the situation before it turned violent. I remember my fear for my dad, and Hank's humiliation. Hank was a victim of WWI, and his story needs to be shared.

What are your stories about?

My stories are about things that actually happened to me. I was born in 1931, on the Minnesota farm that my grandfather purchased in 1876. He broke the prairie sod with oxen. Now, my son has a combine with computers and global positioning, giving us information on the crop yield, the crop's moisture, and the speed of travel; and it has alarms warning us of possible problems as we cover any given acre of land. My stories are about the people who lived through these changing times; the day to day situations that covered their happy days, the difficulties and the tragedies, and the ways they adapted, always heading toward an unknown future.

How did you get started in storytelling?

When I was almost fifty, a brochure came into our home telling of a workshop featuring professional storytellers from New York City. It was to be presented at a college in St. Paul. When I was a young boy, my dad had often said to me, "Cut out those damn stories, and get some work done around here!" I knew that it was not a compliment. I had no idea what to expect at the workshop, but I was drawn by the idea of storytelling as a profession and a healing tool. The first session I attended was interesting, but there was nothing there for me and I planned to leave after lunch. In the cafeteria I sat next to a lady who talked about personal stories, and I decided to stay for the afternoon session. I was surprised to see that she was one of the workshop presenters. She changed my life.

She had each of us present a personal story. As people shared, the stories went from canned humor to total honesty. I learned, that day, that being really listened to, creates a vulnerability and strangers become community.

How long have you been doing it?

From that workshop, a group formed in Minneapolis and met regularly. Most of them were professionals—teachers, actors, or therapists. I was amazed that they made room for me when I attended their gatherings, because my stories were different. They encouraged me to get on the stage when they were invited to speak at a library or a church, and this was totally out of my comfort zone. Eventually, we connected with a group from Chicago, and this opened us up to the national storytelling scene. Along the way, I kept meeting people who helped me to the next rung in the ladder. I've had thirty years of challenge and satisfaction.

Why does a farmer want to get on stage?

Because my father was seventy-three when I graduated from high school, and because my brother was in college, I needed to stay on the farm. In order to keep the farm progressing, I was gradually moved into a management position. When I was in third grade, my teacher had told my mother that I was a "dreamer." I learned, that day, that there was no place on the farm for an artist. About forty years later, storytelling allowed a rebirth for this "dreamer."

The ongoing struggle has been to find the balance between the dreamer and the farmer.

Why do you believe in storytelling?

I am Irish, and I believe the Irish are natural storytellers. But more than that, I believe storytelling has enriched my life in a way that I never dreamed. We need more than one community in our life, and the farming community and storytelling community are so different. But, both farmers and storytellers produce a product from a tiny seed. They depend on faith, dedication, vulnerability and circumstances to reach an uncertain goal.

I find, between the two, that there are more similarities than differences. Storytelling allows me to connect with people that I never would have met, people who were far out of my personal circle. Yet we all have a common bond.

Why do you believe personal stories are healing?

Let me give you an example. John, one of the hoboes who worked on our farm, told the story of wanting to meet a pretty young girl who lived in his neighborhood in the late 1800's. She and her mother drove by his farm on Sundays in their horse and buggy, and he admired her from afar. One

Sunday morning their horse balked by his driveway, and he saw an opportunity to impress her. He grabbed some hay, ran down the driveway, threw it under the horse, and lit it on fire. The horse gave one leap ahead and stopped with the fire now under the buggy. Frantically, John tipped the buggy up on its edge while trying to brush the flames away. The buggy got away from him and rolled into the ditch, along with the girl and her mother. They were not impressed. It was not the outcome John had planned; and when I share that story, it invariably brings stories back to me, often long-hidden stories, where the outcome was not planned. Both the laughter and the tears that accompany these stories bring healing.

What do you think makes a story universal?

People need to hear the story "in their own lives." The teller, and his ego, must disappear.

When the storyteller gets out of the way, the listener is free to connect in his own way. Then the story becomes that person's story, and he is empowered. The listener recognizes the human value that is timeless; and he can see it in his own life, shaping the beginnings of his own story.

What was the highlight of your storytelling career?

The highlight of my storytelling career was the realization that people would actually listen to me. They feed my value back to me; and, somehow, they recognize their own value in my stories.

Where has storytelling taken you?

It has taken me into a much larger world than I ever dreamed. I have spoken at funerals of neighbors and the Smithsonian Celebration of One Hundred Year History of American Agriculture.

I've been on stage with attorney generals and homeless people. I've been on public television, and had my own weekly radio show on a fifty thousand watt radio station. I was featured at the National Storytelling Festival in Jonesborough, Tennessee, and in a healing video used by Mayo Clinic. I have worked with young authors and artists statewide, told my stories at Pete Seeger's festival in New York, and I was the Artistic Director of the Minnesota Storytelling Festival for twenty-two years. It's been a wonderful and unexpected trip.

Do you think you can be both a storyteller and a writer?

I cannot. The story of my life is that I must hire people to do the things that I cannot do. On the farm, there were certain things I was good at; but I am not a mechanic. So, I always had to have a good mechanic working for me. I am good at doctoring cattle, recognizing symptoms and treating them, but when it is a serious problem I always call a veterinarian. So when it came time to write my stories, I knew that I needed to find a writer. I made several attempts, and finally found someone that could write in my "voice."

Then I married her.

What is your hope for the future?

My first hope is that I can stay healthy, and live long enough to keep sharing my stories. We need a world where honesty and truth and vulnerability are featured. We do not find that in this new age of electronics and technology. We have the ability to entertain ourselves. We need to be truly listened to.

If you have enjoyed Michael Cotter's stories,
We invite you to peruse the online catalog at
www.parkhurstbrothers.com